Think
MARKETING

This book is dedicated to the many whose ideas I have borrowed or stolen, especially to those among them whose ideas I have adopted with such enthusiasm or so long ago that I am no longer conscious of my deeds and therefore unable to acknowledge them specifically. The book is also dedicated to the many with whom I have had the pleasure of working and whose efforts, imagination, skills and perseverance have enabled me to develop a few ideas of my own.

Think
MARKETING

Martin van Mesdag
MA, BComm, FInstM, FIMC, FIL

MERCURY BOOKS
Published by W.H. Allen & Co. Plc

First published in 1988
by the Mercury Books Division of
W.H. Allen & Co. Plc
44 Hill Street, London W1X 8LB

Set in Meridien by Phoenix Photosetting, Chatham
Printed and bound in Great Britain by
Mackays of Chatham Ltd, Chatham, Kent

Cartoons by Ken Pyne

British Library Cataloguing in Publication Data

Van Mesdag, Martin
Think marketing.
1. Marketing
I. Title
658.8   HF5415

ISBN 1–85251–095–1

Foreword

Think Marketing is exactly what its title promises. It tries to make its readers think about the purpose of their plans, their decisions, and their actions – to get them to think before they plan, decide, or act. And it does this very nicely.

Marketing is not merely a cluster of related business functions. In a truly marketing-orientated business, marketing is a deeply ingrained attitude of mind, shared by everyone in that business. *Think Marketing* is a practical book. It addresses practitioners. It is written by a man who has been successfully involved in the practice of marketing in many different countries. For many years he was a manager in industry. More recently he has been a consultant. His style is easy and he writes with wit and without jargon.

Martin van Mesdag deals with all the areas which he believes need thought and choices. He revisits old concepts that remain as valid as ever and then adds new dimensions to them – as in the case of the product life-cycle and the marketing mix. Elsewhere he presents new concepts. There is a particularly helpful treatment of the architecture and management of knowledge, where knowledge is treated as a business asset. Van Mesdag has taken the concept of 'global marketing', put two alternative strategies alongside it, and then draws a surprising conclusion. Creativity and know-how are examined in the context of the make-or-buy decision, thus suggesting a reconsideration of a common business practice.

Managers tend to spend most of their time and energy on the problems of the day. When fires rage constantly, firefighting is normal. It can become an all-absorbing occupation. But what about the future? Who looks at that? How should it be done? The *Think Marketing* book shows the way. To read it is to think, and to think is to harness action to the right path.

Theodore Levitt
Edward W. Carter Professor of Business Administration
Editor, *Harvard Business Review*

Introduction

> He (the chief executive) has to know precisely where he himself wants to go, and make sure the whole organization is enthusiastically aware of where that is. This is a first requisite of leadership, for *unless he knows where he is going, any road will take him there.* If any road is okay, the chief executive may as well pack his attaché case and go fishing. If an organization does not know or care where it is going, it does not need to advertise the fact with a ceremonial figurehead.
>
> Theodore Levitt: 'Marketing Myopia',
> *Harvard Business Review*, July–August, 1960

It is not surprising that Professor Levitt's phrase, italicized above, has acquired much fame. Travel without a destination may not be all that prevalent, but activity in business without thought about its purpose or future is horrifyingly commonplace. This book is about the need to think and the things to think about. In an ever-faster-changing business environment, unless we ensure that thought precedes action, panic will replace thought.

The purpose of thinking before acting is twofold. First, it reduces the risk of an all-absorbing succession of firefighting exercises and a helter-skelter course to a writhing demise. Secondly, it provides the challenge of shaping the future of one's enterprise and holds out the opportunity of both collective and individual accomplishment.

So the message is – brain first, feet second.

To think, to think ahead (of action), does not come naturally to many people. Yet it is not all that difficult. Whilst some techniques and methods used in marketing are difficult, the important issues tend to be simple. Just because something is difficult does not mean that mastery of it confers wisdom. On the rare occasion when one meets wisdom, it is nearly always based on straightforward, simple principles. Having expressed this heartfelt opinion, I hasten to disclaim any element of wisdom in what you will read in this book, much as I wish it could be otherwise. This book does not present irrefutable truisms. It does not present both sides of arguments. Often as not the reasoning behind the ideas presented is omitted. There are no ifs and buts and no 'on-the-one-hand' and 'on-the-other'. What the book presents will turn out to be meat to one person and toxin to another.

So be it. I am setting out not to please you, not to persuade you towards my point of view (much as I should like you to share it), but only to make you think: to make you think about things I know to be important for the destiny of your business, to think about the people with some sort of stake in it – which includes you yourself. It is my dear wish that I may set in motion, if only once or twice, thoughts in your mind which – with your knowledge of your business environment – will be of benefit to the community of which you are part: your company.

The recurring use of the first person singular has, as its sole function, to reflect the individuality of the views presented.

At the end of most chapters there are a few questions which the reader may find it useful to ponder and discuss with others in his company or against which he may care to weigh his own views.

Think Marketing makes the case that thought about action and plans for action in marketing ought to be part of every marketing man's life and that, moreover, the fruitfulness of that thought is greatly enhanced by open and frequent communication between people at all levels of management in business organizations. Accordingly the book is addressed to marketing practitioners at every level of management, including that at which the incumbent has outgrown the first-hand responsibility for day-to-day marketing operations. The book is not written for professors of marketing (flattered as I would be to know of any that read it!), but should be of use to those students who are set upon a career in the practice of marketing.

It is my firm belief that there are far too few women in marketing. A woman's perceptiveness and sensitivity, her style of reasoning and her conscientiousness are attributes that are vital to the management of marketing. Quite apart from this, women rather than men, in many markets, are customers and that qualifies women rather than men for careers in marketing. I express this view not just because I hope lots of women will read this book but because in it I do something which must not be taken at face value. I use 'man' to mean 'man or woman'. To write 'man or woman' every time would make for tedious reading.

This book comes without a glossary. There is no need for one. Jargon

is avoided, and where marketing terms are used their precise definition doesn't matter (worse, could mislead or lead to entirely useless
argument), though their broad meaning will emerge from the text.

There are lots of practical examples of the subjects under discussion.
Mostly the sources of these examples are identified, either because the
people concerned have allowed me to do so or because they themselves have made the material public at some previous occasion. In a
minority of instances my examples have had to remain anonymous.

Most of any knowledge I may have of marketing has been gained in
consumer product markets, much of it in food and drink marketing. I
make this statement as a caveat to the reader, more than an apology.

I do not believe that great and lasting success in marketing can be
achieved only through brilliance. Brilliant ideas are great when you
can get them, and help a business to be successful. But the things that
matter most in consistently successful marketing are really quite
simple. It is with those that *Think Marketing* aims to deal. The book
begins and ends with chapters about competition and competitiveness.
Those are not things to suit everybody or for which everybody is
suited. Some will think, with Henry David Thoreau:

Why should we be in such desperate haste to succeed in such
desperate enterprises? If a man does not keep pace with his com-
panions, perhaps it is because he hears a different drummer. Let him
step to the music which he hears, however measured or far away.

Well, this book is about haste and enterprise. I hope the drummer
comes through unmuffled.

Acknowledgements

This book comes without a bibliography, because one would have looked conspicuous for its brevity. It would simply have said 'writings by Peter Drucker, Ted Levitt and John Argenti'. It is those three people, more than any others, who have enabled me over many years to get some sort of order into the thinking behind my work, and so it is to them that I am indirectly indebted for the contents of this book. Professor Levitt I should also like to thank for his direct encouragement in the writing process.

I wish to express admiration for the thoughts, the work and the expressive ability of the many who are quoted in the text to highlight or exemplify the subject matter I am trying to put across.

I am grateful to the many companies (and the individuals in them) who have modelled in order to illustrate, amplify or clarify points made in my text.

I acknowledge Barclays Bank (Chapter 1), Harvard Business School (Chapter 4), *Campaign* (Chapter 13), the *Financial Times* (Chapter 15), and *Fortune* (Chapters 14 and 16) as sources for material or ideas I have used.

The following publications have let me use bits from articles I wrote for them: *Tijdschrift voor Marketing* (Chapter 6), *Financial Economisch Magazine* (Chapter 5), *Harvard Business Review* (Chapter 6), *Management* (Chapter 8), *Absatzwirtschaft* (Chapter 9), *Chief Executive* (Chapters 8 and 9), *Marketing Week* (Chapter 11), *Marketing* (Chapter 12), *Management Today* (Chapter 15), and *Het Financieele Dagblad* (Chapters 15 and 16).

I am tremendously grateful to Sir Adrian Cadbury, Professor Michael Baker and Mr Michael Rines for reading the manuscript and giving me their comments.

Finally, my very warm thanks to Nuala (my wife), Bronwen Wolton and Susie Hunter-Blair for their very many suggestions as to language, style and content, and to Bronwen for committing the whole lot to disc.

Contents

1

Shopping at Britain Ltd

Britain is a nation, not so much of shopkeepers anymore, but of frustrated shoppers.

Napoleon Bonaparte (updated by author)

WHERE ARE WE NOW?

This book tries to identify subjects, concepts and ideas which it seems useful to think about for people who are interested in improving the competitiveness of their companies. In thinking ahead it is useful to know accurately where we are today – hence the above heading. But the picture of today is not static, it is one shot in the film of time and that shot did not come about by accident: just as it will be related to what we want to happen in the future, so it is related to what did happen in the past. In planning for the future we cannot ignore the past because many of the trends of the past will have gained the inertia to propel them into the future. Therefore, if in the picture of today there is evidence of trends in the past and if those should be trends we want to reverse, divert or circumvent, we had better know what those trends are and what measure of inertia has built up in them.

The picture of today as drawn in these pages is neither flattering nor kind; some of the assessments made will be perceived as harsh. The stance in this chapter, one of self-criticism, is taken in the belief that such an attitude is a condition for any constructive measures to improve the competitiveness of British business.

Some – I hope the most important – dimensions in terms of which today's marketing environment may be depicted follow under the ensuing headings. Comparatively little space is given to the first, Britain's economic performance, since it already has been, and continues to be, well documented in a host of publications which appear almost daily.

[1]

BRITAIN'S ECONOMIC PERFORMANCE

In Britain we tend to apply standards selected for their ability to flatter our performance rather than for their objectivity. If Britain takes part in an international sporting event, our media will provide us with a detailed account of the performance of those of the competing athletes who came in fifth and fourth in order to justify the headline treatment for the man from Britain who came third. The two who won the race and came second are not mentioned at all. If the international exchange rate of our currency is on a long-term downward slide, we compare it with a well known currency which is also sliding down, and so, every evening on television, we are told how sterling is doing against the dollar. When we consider the health of our industries (profitability, growth rates, productivity, investment, R & D activity, etc.) it is compared with its less healthy state 3 years earlier, not with how it stacks up against our international competitors. So we live on in our blissful insularity. From this I must, however briefly, rouse the reader by submitting just a few internationally geared yardsticks.

In 1900 Britain had 34 per cent of world exports of manufactured goods; the USA had 12 per cent, Germany 22 per cent, France 15 per cent, Italy 3 per cent and Japan 2 per cent. By the early 1980s the shares of the USA, West Germany and Japan were each hovering in the region of 17 per cent, and France, Italy and the UK in the region of 7 per cent. In 1980 the difference between UK exports and imports of manufactured goods – the country's trade balance – was positive (i.e. exports were worth more) to the tune of £3.7 billion. By 1986 that balance had deteriorated to a negative value of £6.6 billion.

The overall trade balance is the result of adding positive bilateral trade balances with some countries and deducting negative bilateral balances with others. What is especially worrying is that the negative balances tend to be with countries offering large, affluent markets (mainly West Germany, Japan, Italy, USA, France, Switzerland and the Benelux countries), wheras our bilateral trade surpluses are earned in countries that do not offer such lush pickings (Saudi Arabia, South Africa, Australia, Nigeria, Iran, Ireland and Russia are the main ones in this category).*

As if this situation is not already bad enough, it does not stand alone. Almost without exception, the currencies of the desirable countries with whom Britain has negative trade balances are the very ones

* House of Lords Select Committee on Overseas Trade Report.

against which the pound sterling has not risen but fallen the most!

The purchasing power of the pound in 1950 was almost at the 1920 level, but by 1986 it had dropped to 8½ per cent of the 1920 value. The position of the pound in relation to other currencies provides an even more sombre picture of how those exchange rates have changed from 1950 to (January) 1987. In Table 1.1 the other currencies' units per pound in 1987 are shown as a percentage of the number of units per pound in 1950.

In the light of these figures, what is absolutely mind-boggling is that the third quarter 1986 survey by the UK Chambers of Commerce reveals the high exchange value of sterling to be the second most serious impediment to an improvement in business performance!

International trade, especially in manufactured products, has risen phenomenally, and one country's exports are another country's imports. Britain is one of quite a number of developed countries (the United States leads the world in this troublesome listing) whose imports exceed exports and who therefore have negative trade bal-

TABLE 1.1   Movement of pound against other currencies, 1950–87 (per cent)*

Foreign currencies weakening against £		Foreign currencies rising against £	
Finnish Markka	93.6	Australian Dollar	109.6
Greek Drachma	20.8	Austrian Schilling	308.6
Irish Punt	96.2	Belgian Franc	244.9
Italian Lira	88.8	Canadian Dollar	146.3
New Zealand Dollar	71.9	Danish Krone	184.6
Nigerian Naira	35.3	French Franc	106.0
Portuguese Escudo	37.6	German Mark	424.6
South African Rand	63.5	Hong Kong Dollar	136.4
Spanish Peseta	56.7	Japanese Yen	434.9
		Malaysian Ringgit	224.3
		Dutch Guilder	339.9
		Norwegian Krone	187.3
		Singapore Dollar	265.3
		Swedish Krona	146.6
		Swiss Franc	513.2
		US Dollar	185.4
		(yes, US Dollar!)	

The very high sterling interest rates have not prevented this slide.

*Barclays Bank.

ances. The most obvious ways of curing negative trade balances are curtailing imports or boosting exports. For the boosting of exports there is only one remedy, which is also very effective in curbing imports: it is more effective marketing. For the reduction of imports there is a totally different cure, which works instantly, is incompatible with the first remedy, and in the longer term will attack exports: it is protective measures enforced by the state. What is wrong with that method is that it does nothing to improve the competitiveness of the protected domestic supplier and it provokes retaliatory protective measures by the insensitive governments of countries where our exports go.

Successful exporting obviously is helped by the unlimited availability of something which everybody wants, such as diamonds, grain, sea-sun-and-sand, energy or tea. But it is also helped by being orientated towards the needs of foreign customers.

Even in a closely knit group of countries like the European Community this export orientation leads to enormous differences in relative export performance. See Table 1.2.

The only conclusion I would venture to draw from these numbers is that the three countries whose export value exceeds half of their GDP are all small countries (see Chapter 5 The World Is Our Market). When you meet the business people from those countries, their export-orientated attitudes are immediately obvious.

The figures from Tables 1.1 and 1.2, and the many other gloomy ones from which this book spares the reader, are great for politicians, economists and public speakers, but they do little to spur industry on to

TABLE 1.2   Export value in per cent of Gross Domestic Product, 1985*

Belgium and Luxemburg	66
Denmark	30
France	19
West Germany	30
Greece	14
Ireland	57
Italy	22
Netherlands	56
Portugal	29
Spain	14
United Kingdom	23

*Barclays Bank.

do something about it. If such figures were to be much more widely publicized, it is still doubtful whether that would have much effect. Appeals are frequently made, mostly by politicians, to the business community to contribute to an improvement in the country's economic performance. The patriotism of businessmen does not, however, appear to stretch far enough for those appeals to be heeded.

Fortunately the performance of the economy as a whole does not imply the setting of a standard. Any individual enterprise can decide it wants to do better.

ANTI-BUSINESS CULTURE

Despite the fact that Britain was the first country to have an industrial revolution, despite the circumstance that Britain used to be a major trading nation, despite the fact that Britain has played (and to a considerable extent still does play) an important role in the world marketplace for such services as banking and insurance, Britain's culture has always been and it still is anti-business. There appears to be an inbred belief that there is something indecent and dishonest about business; and, within business, the closer one gets to the selling end of enterprise, the more disreputable one is perceived to be. The professions are where people should strive to be, the armed forces are perfectly respectable, the church is OK, teaching is very worthy, and farming, though not respectable, is at least honest. But business is perceived as a wholly undesirable pursuit.

The country's education system provides little exposure to the business world, and, where it does do so, it is often strongly anti-business. Business has extreme difficulty hiring a fair proportion of the most intelligent students graduating from colleges and universities. Members of the Royal Family are generally groomed for military careers, not business.

Society, presumably, and the media, certainly, express the view that business should become aware of its social responsibility, should show greater concern for the environment, should behave more honestly and openly and should show more restraint in the exercise of its financial muscle. That criticism is understandable and much of it is justified, but to fail to point to the enormous benefits to society from business, to fail to point to the massive deceit people have to put up with from other institutions, such as local and national government, the mismanagement they suffer from at the hands of local and national authority administrators and the wholesale bias bestowed on people by the media themselves are omissions which do nothing but mislead.

RICHES THROUGH TIME

Most rich nations display their wealth through the amounts of money spent both by the state and by individuals. The nice thing about all that spending is that most of it eventually goes to other people, so that they can get rich too.

But it would be taking too narrow a view to suggest that wealth is only displayed by the free and easy way people spend money. One

One rich nation chooses to play with time.

extremedly rich nation does not indulge in the free and easy spending
of money. It deliberately and with dedication chooses to display its
wealth in another way. It does it through the way it plays with *time*.
That country is the UK. None of the countries with which Britain
competes can afford quite such luxurious treatment of time as Britons
enjoy. Britons come to work an hour (or more) later than the citizens
of other Western nations. No other country luxuriates in a fortnight of
annual Christmas paralysis (the time when domestic demand for
many goods and services reaches its peak). Nowhere are wages so
universally and directly linked to the number of hours a person is
present at his place of employment (rather than to the amount and
quality of work delivered) than in Britain, and nowhere is an individual's discretionary time held in higher esteem; any attempt at
encroachment upon it meets with violent opposition. In Britain people
speak about 'overtime', but in other countries the term is 'overwork'
(and it has nothing to do with being overworked). Not unreasonably,
work is perceived by Britons as an inevitable interference with one's
time. There is widespread endeavour to find ways of reducing the time
spent at work, in contrast with other rich countries, whose different
criteria for the accumulation of wealth prompts people to look for
ways of increasing the amount of money derived from work.

It is not for me to impose harsh judgements on either the one or the
other criterion for the measurement of wealth, but the plain and
inescapable fact is that an individual, a company of individuals or a
nation of individuals must make a choice between them. The two are in
conflict with one another: striving for maximum money is irreconcila-
ble with striving for maximum time. It is unrealistic therefore, and in
fact deceitful, to tell a nation which has demonstrated its addiction to
wealth in time that it can emulate the material wealth of another nation
which has accustomed itself to measuring its wealth in money. The
likelihood of being able to change the attitude of a whole nation is
exceedingly remote and the desirability of bringing about such a change
must be questioned. However, if the general attitude in the land is to
continue to strive for wealth in time, there is no compelling need for any
single individual or indeed for any given company of individuals to
conform to that attitude. To strive for monetary wealth is altogether
possible, and the choice to sacrifice time for money is open to anyone. If
such a choice is made by a business enterprise, it is one that must be
made consciously and it must be shared by every individual who is part
of that enterprise, You cannot have people with fundamentally
different motivations working together towards the same goals.

INTERESTING AND CIVILIZED

A popular pastime – millions all over the world indulge in it – is for the people of one nation to ascribe a package of attributes to the people of another nation. The attributes doled out to the citizens of another nation are not necessarily all negative; the practice seems to be that it is all right for the combined attributes ascribed to the inhabitants of another country to be favourable as long as they are less so than the totality of attributes awarded to one's own people.

The pastime results in comments starting with 'Typically French . . .', 'Italians never have . . .' and 'The American habit of . . .'

Among the citizens of any one nation there tends to be an easily reached consensus about the typical characteristics of any particular nationality, the more readily so the less first-hand knowledge those making the judgement have of those they are judging. There is a simple reason for this. Ascribing attributes to the people from another country is not done after assiduous study and analysis of the foreigners in question. Rather, these attributes are ascribed on the basis of where and how, after superficial and hasty examination, the foreigners' behaviour differs from one's own. What is obtained by this process is a sort of negative mirror image. The typification which results from this process has little value. Ask an Italian and a Belgian for their opinion of 'The French' and two radically different descriptions emerge. The typical Englishman as perceived by the Dutch is so utterly unlike the English as perceived by the Irish that you wonder how the two could share the same planet.

I have just argued that cross-border judgements by one people of another are invalid. Yet, of course, there are things about the culture in any one country which set it apart from others. History, climate, government, education, the economics, the topography of the country, the soil and what it is capable of producing, its relations with other nations, all these things help to shape a country's culture; and a country's culture – the standards and criteria people use, the values they hold, the expectations they have of each other's behaviour – affects their life-styles (and their business styles!). So, conscious of the extreme danger of doing so, let me examine British society and any effects the nation's culture has upon the way it conducts business.

What makes Britain attractive is the circumstance that it is a colourful society. Extremes in every field of human endeavour are greater in Britain than in any other developed country. It doesn't matter where one looks, whether in the arts, education, religion, industry, the professions, the communities in which people live, the clothes they wear, the things they eat, their spare-time activities, there is a broader spectrum of variations and there are greater extremes than are found in other countries.

In most normal countries having to live with such extremes would arouse in the people living there the urge to bash each other's heads in. Not so in Britain. The British can cope with these extremes without widespread resort to manslaughter. Indeed many British people take pleasure in the divergencies, contrasts, and eccentricities in the society of which they are part. Britons can cope because they possess two related qualities. Firstly, Britons are very loath to interfere with their fellow citizens. Britons regard each other as individuals each surrounded by a neatly fenced spiritual garden – you do not trespass into his garden and he doesn't into yours. If you address each other, it is only by express common consent, it is across the fence and at arm's length. (This explains the great popularity of the weather as a subject of conversation.) The other quality is one of the noblest to which the people of any nation could hope to aspire: it is tolerance.

Being accustomed to wide-ranging variations in everything, reluctance to interfere with one another and great tolerance are the attributes which typify British people. They are attributes which go to make the most interesting and the most civilized of Western cultures.

BAD FOR BUSINESS

Those same laudable attributes, however, do have their dark sides. Nowhere do those dark sides come to the fore more obviously than in business, more especially in marketing.

Are the British bad at marketing? The answer has to be no. Britain's marketing insights are widely admired abroad, even in the United States. Britons are asked to speak and write about marketing in every country of the world. British marketing practices are frequently held up as shining examples in other countries. In terms of business volume and student numbers the Institute of Marketing in Britain is the largest in the world. It is also, without doubt, the most influential.

British advertising (and that includes the work done by Britons in American-owned advertising agencies) is of a very high standard and ranks with the very best in the world. A disproportionately large part of the best industrial, package and graphic design in the world comes

Individuals, each surrounded by a neatly fenced spiritual garden.

from British designers. Spending on marketing research (as measured against sales) is higher than almost anywhere else in the world; not only that, but the UK research professionalism is unequalled and it is not surprising that the British marketing research industry has experienced very substantial expansion abroad.

Having identified these strengths of British marketing, it is only fair to point out that British industry generally does not distinguish itself from the industries in other countries by being strongly marketing-orientated. Strong marketing orientation in the industry of any developed country remains the exception rather than the rule, and there is nothing very exceptional about Britain in this respect.

Earlier, I mentioned the dark sides of marketing in Britain and how these were related to typical attributes of British people. There are two specific elements:

1. Selling is very difficult for Britons.

2. Britons have compassion for 'poor old Fred'.

Let us consider the first point. The fear of crossing the fence into the spiritual garden of another, or reticence to intrude upon another's privacy, makes the British wary of invading another man's life, including the other man's business life. The British salesman has to overcome a reluctance to discuss his customer's business with him, and he is averse to applying himself to the task of learning everything about his customer's business and the market it serves.*

The training of British salesmen, to the extent that it takes place at all, does not adequately address itself specifically to these two problems. Bad training produces foot-in-the-door salesmanship; relatively good training appears to focus on the art of making sales presentations – which is all right as far as it goes, but it doesn't address itself to the development of communicative skills and the acquisition of customer knowledge to overcome the inherent inhibitions of the British salesman. Without development and training of this kind selling will not become what should become the dedication of every salesman: helping customers to buy.

Secondly, as regards the tolerance of the British, that admirable

---

* Boston Consulting Group, Institute of Marketing, NEDO, Barclays Bank International, AGS Management Consultants, Institute of Purchasing and Supply, Sussex University Science Policy Research Unit, and Gallup have all conducted or commissioned research programmes which highlight these weaknesses.

tolerance unfortunately extends to tolerance of the under-performance of individuals, groups of people, and civic and business organizations. Among the developed nations, only Britons tolerate dirty hospitals, haphazard train connections, inadequate highways and ever-worsening communication services. With incredible for-bearance Britons accept late (or non-) deliveries, sub-standard qual-ity, out-of-stocks, wrong specifications, premature breakdowns and inadequate servicing. Britons accept 'we will do/have done our best' as an adequate excuse for the abominable performance of a supplier, and order from that supplier again; and Britons will soothe themselves and others by saying 'Poor old Fred; he did try' when the despicable Fred sends an invoice for a transaction in which he miserably failed to perform.

IS FRED UNFAIR?

Now one could argue 'So what? If people are happy that way, why not leave them to it?' There are two responses. Firstly, it is grossly unfair, if not downright dishonest, to charge prices, rates, taxes or contributions for goods or services which are not or improperly delivered. The second response is even more serious. Tolerance of under-performance breeds under-performance. In not a few instances under-performance has become the norm. In 1986 British Rail was under-performing. The corporation hired advertising space to say so: 'We're getting there', it said, which means we are not there now. In a more detailed advertisement BR identified nine specific areas in which it knew itself to be under-performing. These ranged from discourteous staff and cancelled trains to rundown stations and delayed train arri-vals. In that advertisement the corporation spelt out how it aimed to make improvements in (rather than remedy) each of those areas. The closing line of the advertisement ran: 'We can't guarantee achieving these aims everywhere all the time, but we can promise 100% effort in trying to do so'.

   I do not know what effect the advertising campaign had. The fact that it did not run very long may have meant that BR were dis-appointed. Notwithstanding my earlier laudatory comments on British advertising, I consider this campaign bad advertising. What is interesting, and illustrates the point I am trying to make, is that BR and its advertising agency obviously believed in the campaign and con-

British Rail's new positive attitude towards the South-East.

NO less than 90% of trains running in the Network to arrive on or within five minutes of the scheduled time.

NO more than 1% of commuter trains running in the South-East having to be cancelled, for whatever reason.

NO litter cluttering up train interiors.

NO rundown, unkempt stations anywhere in the Network.

NO trains to arrive at your station in the morning without having received an exterior wash and an interior clean.

NO need to stand on any peak-time train for more than 20 minutes.

NO lengthy queues at ticket offices.

NO long waits on the telephone trying to get through to enquiries.

NO member of staff to be anything other than courteous and co-operative should you require help.

NO we can't guarantee achieving these aims everywhere, all the time, but we can promise 100% effort in trying to do so.

≥ Network SouthEast

Campaign in the Poor Old Fred vein.

sidered it good – initially at any rate. But the whole campaign as well as the quoted ad was in the Poor Old Fred vein!

COMPETITIVENESS

I believe that lack of competitiveness, under-performance – call it what you like – is not merely unbusinesslike, but economically, socially and morally wrong. I should be immensely pleased if, in the pages which follow, I might succeed in triggering one or two thoughts in the reader's mind which will lead to action that enhances the competitiveness of his company.

2

How Far Does 'Marketing' Go?

If not the concept, then the term – at any rate – has been around for well over a century. My 'new' edition of *Webster's Dictionary* of 1880 says:

> **Mär'ket-ing,** n.   1. The act of purchasing in market
> 2. Articles in market; supplies

NO DEFINITIONS

This is the only marketing book in which there are no definitions of the concept of 'marketing'. Definitions are avoided because there are so many, and therefore one becomes embroiled in having to evaluate the relative merits of each. Such an exercise has no practical value. 'Marketing' and many of the concepts within it (take 'merchandising', 'sales promotion' or 'publicity') defy precise definition, and how anyone chooses to define it does not matter much.

What does matter a great deal is that a number of functions, disciplines and thinking routines should be so organized and managed in an enterprise that they will interact logically, fruitfully, harmoniously, creatively, profitably and lastingly. In no area of managerial endeavour is this interaction more crucial than in marketing. Chapter 4, headed 'The Marketing Mix', is dedicated to it.

At the root of 'marketing' lies the characteristic that the whole is more powerful than the sum of its constituent parts. If 'marketing' works the way it should, then two plus two is five, not four. When this is the case, the constituent parts have synergy with one another.

'Marketing' encompasses a number of distinct and different management entities which have two fundamental characteristics in common: first, they are directly aimed at fulfilling the purpose and objectives of the business and, second, they are linked together by a central plan and central management.

[15]

MARKETING ORIENTATION

In practice, 'marketing' encompasses a widely varying assortment of management activities, and the breadth of that assortment in a given company gives an indication of the marketing orientation of the enterprise in question. The degree of marketing orientation of a business matters. The more marketing-orientated a company is, the more directly will it be applying itself to its purpose and objectives, the more positively will it be geared to having and holding customers, and the more widespread – within the organization – the benefits of synergy will be. It is useful therefore to examine the various stages of marketing orientation as we find them in the real world of business.

1. The mixed bag

This is commonly found in companies in which certain functions have emerged but have not thus far found a home. These functions are, say, marketing research, advertising and sales promotion. The people engaged upon these tasks are then lumped together and called the marketing department. That department may or may not have one man called the marketing manager, and he may be expected to report to the sales director or the managing director or (Heaven help the poor unfortunate!) to both. Product development, pricing, distribution, customer servicing and public relations would be housed elsewhere, undoubtedly under several other functional headings.

The main effort in this configuration goes into defensive battles for autonomy between the departments among which the various bits of marketing responsibility have been parcelled out. That crucial attribute of marketing – synergy – does not get a chance. The company in question in fact is concerned with marketing in name only.

If the company survives this phase, it will eventually discover that the marketing department as it was conceived doesn't work, and temporary solace is found by adding to the mixed bag one of the marketing constituents hitherto left out of it. Invariably this is selling, it having become obvious that a solution for the continuous tussles between sales and what is called marketing must be found.

The solution is just a palliative, for whilst it may solve some of the wasteful battles between the two departments, the combined function is still a limbless body unable to make marketing work for the business. Operationally it is a nonsensical solution. This configuration is often

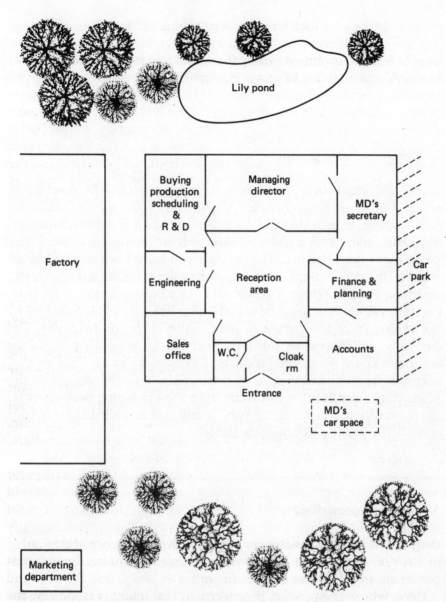

Lily pond

Factory

Buying
production
scheduling
&
R & D

Managing
director

MD's
secretary

Engineering

Reception
area

Finance &
planning

Car
park

Sales
office

W.C.

Cloak
rm

Accounts

Entrance

MD's
car space

Marketing
department

The company is concerned with marketing in name only.

labelled 'Marketing and Sales' (or 'Sales and Marketing') in deference
to the sales people, who have been around for a long time and whom it
would be unkind to rob of their identity.

Sales and marketing (or its inverse) conceptually too is nonsensical. However much one may argue about the inclusion of some of the more peripheral functional areas under the marketing banner, sales is first and foremost among those that indisputably belong there. Marketing and sales is like fruit and apples.

2. Unimpeachable product

In this case 'marketing', or what in a company that fits this description passes for marketing, includes all the functions which obviously belong there, except that the company's product is a given quantity. Marketing starts with a given product over whose nature or attributes it can exert no influence. The product will have been devised by an engineering department, a manufacturing department, a research and development laboratory, a design office or a buying department. During its development, the product will have been closely scrutinized by the chairman of the company (and, quite likely, by his wife). The company will regard its business function as 'producing shoes' or sealing wax or whatever products it decides to make. But in that decision, in the attributes, the construction and the design of the product, no contribution has come from the marketing people. As far as the marketing department (yes, it will still be called that) is concerned, the product is unimpeachable.

3. Category-prescribed

Only in this phase are we beginning to see the emergence of marketing in any real sense. More fast moving packaged-consumer-goods companies are in this phase than in any other.

Here, where the product is concerned, marketing is made responsible for product formulation, pack design, pricing and testing (along with other marketing functions). The product category (-ies) in which the company operates, however, is (are) not at the discretion of marketing people. Marketing in this category of companies is not given the responsibility of finding new product opportunities in response to which the company might diversify. Like the cobbler, the marketing people are confined to their last.

4. Market-prescribed

In this phase the company has decided to confine its energies to one (or several) specific market(s) and marketing has been given comprehensive responsibility for the company's business in that (those) market(s) – whether the market is a country (Outer Mongolia), a trade (chemists), an industry (electronics manufacturers), or a category of end-users (primary-school teachers or overweight women).

Here marketing has the opportunity to develop wholly new products or services, or to buy in products for (assembly and) resale. Marketing is given the challenge of optimizing the company's business in that given market, but it is denied the opportunity of finding synergistic benefits from serving allied or adjoining markets.

5. SWOT-based

The most advanced stage of marketing orientation a company can aspire to goes a long step further. It is where the responsibilities of marketing are constrained only by what the company has defined as its objectives, its mission and its policy. In companies which have developed to this advanced stage of marketing orientation the influence of marketing becomes evident from strategy-making onwards. Marketing starts with an analysis of the SWOT (Strengths, Weaknesses, Opportunities, Threats) of the company and its environment as a whole, and has total responsibility for the selection of both markets and products. One can argue that in such an advanced stage of marketing orientation Marketing is in fact doing the job of general management. There is no doubt that in companies of this kind marketing attitudes have become deeply ingrained in the thinking of managers in every functional area of the business. There is no doubt either that in the determination of corporate objectives, mission and policy, marketing chiefs will have exerted their influence. But it would be wrong to assume that marketing would of necessity encroach upon the development and management of such other resources and functions as people, finance, manufacturing, engineering or procurement, or upon the style and standards the company adopts.

This advanced positioning of marketing in business practice is as yet fairly rare. I believe it will become more common. It is this kind of positioning of marketing in companies which is the basis for this book.

ADVANCED

The successive stages described in this chapter have been dubbed increasingly 'advanced' degrees of marketing orientation. Since the use of the word suggests that the successive states are increasingly desirable, the choice of wording might be questioned.

I believe the five phases describing an advancement in marketing orientation do suggest successive improvements in the running of a business, for two straightforward reasons:

1. The descreasing conflict and the increasing synergies inherent in this advancement are of direct and obvious benefit to the business as a whole.

2. As providers of revenue, customers are a unique group of people. The closer the more people in the company can get to an understanding of customers and the greater the harmony between them as they do so, the more likely that revenue will grow.

In the next chapter we look a little more closely at people, recognizing that it is people who are the primary assets any business can strive to build.

QUESTIONS

1. Of the five phases of marketing orientation described, which is the closest to where your company stands?

2. Is the company's degree of marketing orientation as it now stands deliberately chosen or has it got there by accident?

3. Do you want to change the company's marketing orientation? If so, how and why?

3

People

Most people, whether men or women, wish above all else to be comfortable, and thought is pre-eminently an uncomfortable process.

Vera Brittain: *Testament of Youth*

'STAKEHOLDERS'

Business is people first and foremost. There are distinctly different groups of people that have some sort of relation with a business enterprise. Each of those groups of people has a specific interest in that business enterprise and the interest of one group is quite different from, and may be diametrically opposed to, the interest of another group. The groups comprise owners, employees, suppliers, traders, members of the public, moneylenders (to include people who might be prospective members of any of these groups) and government (local, national and international). There is of course a further group, and so this is a good place to point to where *it* differs from the groups I have enumerated. All the ones I have mentioned at one time or another expect to get money or their money's worth from the company, whether by way of dividends, wages, remittances, margins, environmental protection schemes or taxes. The further group is unique in that it *pays* money to the company. I refer to customers. That unique quality of customers endears them to business people, gives them prime status among all the groups I have mentioned, and explains their royal class (as in 'the customer is king').

The decisions and choices of *all* these groups of people determine whether the business enterprise they relate to will survive. The business can, and indeed must, make propositions, but the decision-takers on whom the survival of the business wholly depends are those groups of people who are mostly outside.

A unique group in that they actually pay money to the company.

To put it negatively but without exaggeration, if *any* of these groups of people should decide they want to bring the business down, they can do so. It sometimes happens: for example, public sentiment has caused dozens of foreign businesses to close their doors in South Africa; banks kill bright, commercial initiatives because they are unable to assess risks; and traders bring companies down through sustained loss-leading of their wares and destroying their brands. Even shareholders have ruined their own companies by draining them of cash through their greedy insistence on dividends rather than using profits to build equity.

Some refer to all these groups of people as 'stakeholders'. It is a term which must not be taken too literally, but it does describe the intrinsic relation of people (mainly) on the outside with the business and it hints strongly at the idea that a company had better look after its relations with these groups of people, or else. . . !

There was a time when marketing people thought they could confine their attention to the simultaneous satisfaction of the needs of customers and shareholders. This is not so now. No one in any company, least of all marketing people, can ignore the interests, desires, expectations, requirements or criticisms which come from any of its stakeholders. Here are illustrations of how marketing effectiveness can stem directly from the keen observation of what is in the minds of other groups of stakeholders.

- The early 1970s was when health foods were still largely the concern of young women without make-up in purple skirts and young men with beads, beards and sandals. But the word was beginning to spread beyond these pioneers, and from the way the press and subsequently the television media were exposing the issue it was clear (then!) that healthy eating rather than health foods stood to become a very major issue in the UK. Food manufacturers and retailers would benefit from an early response to those signals. Some did.

- Legislation controlling such things as taxation, labelling, product composition, advertising and selling does not come about suddenly. Even the conception of such legislation can take years. The authorities working on legislation tend to be very accessible and so it is quite feasible to get advance warning of legislation which will affect marketing operations. In not a few cases it is possible to influence the law-making process and thereby forestall the most damaging aspects of it.

- One of the most obvious groups of stakeholders a timely insight
  into whose attitudes may prevent missed orders, lost customers
  and a lot of unpleasantness is employees.

- Moneylenders tend to withdraw their support at the very
  moment that orders are coming into the borrower's business at
  an unprecedented rate. An insight into the minds and workings
  of moneylenders may well prevent such an occurrence; they
  respond favourably to detailed schedules and plans and will
  tolerate wide-ranging contingencies provided they are presented
  in great detail and with actuarial accuracy.

- Early awareness of causes promulgated by vociferous groupings
  among the general public, even if they are very small minorities,
  is essential. Early-warning signs will help the company to choose
  a course to avoid confrontation. An early understanding of such
  causes may well lead to better business in a better world. We got
  safer cars that way, plus better advertising, cleaner direct-mail
  practices, healthier food products, and a cleaner and better
  looking environment.

One group of people I have not enumerated is competitors, first,
because attaching the word 'stakeholder' to a competitor might be
perceived as pushing things a bit far, and secondly, and much more
importantly, because in its relations with just about every one of the
groups a company is in competition with others. A company meets
competitors not just in the marketplace. A company competes with
others in finding good employees (and in holding on to those it has
got), in finding suppliers (of some goods and services more than
others), in winning public acceptance, in obtaining approval of development plans, or in borrowing money.

I would not for an instant suggest that customers are not the first
group of people marketing men should be concerned with or that the
interests of shareholders are not their second concern. But those very
concerns make it imperative that the interests, attitudes, grievances,
aims, anxieties and beliefs of all other groups or stakeholders are
perceived and considered by marketing men and, wherever this is in
the interests of the company as a whole, that measures are taken or
actions avoided to accommodate these symptoms.

THE COMPANY'S PERSONALITY

Every group of stakeholders expects a certain pattern of behaviour from the company. In due course stakeholders will endow the company with a personality, shaped by the stakeholder's perceptions of what the company is, does or does not do. There may be differences between the stakeholder's expectations and his actual perceptions. The company may feel those differences are undesirable and it may decide to do something about them. An imperative requirement for the personality of a company is that it is consistent. Inconsistencies in its behaviour or attitudes will very quickly cause it to be labelled untrustworthy, devious and unreliable. Consistency, however, is very hard to bring about.

Comparisons between the behaviours of human beings and organizations – not least business organizations – have often been and will continue to be made. Making such comparisons is a relatively harmless pursuit as long as their limitation is recognized. You cannot make comparisions in every respect and there are two important reasons why:

1. Humans are mortal, but business organizations, generally speaking, are expected to last; in fact they are expected to prosper and grow continuously.

2. Each human being has his own personality and, whilst he may decide to work on that personality, most people don't; they expect to be taken as they are. A business is a group of people, each with his own individual characteristics.

Because of the diversity of personalities of the people in the business and, moreover, because each of those people sooner or later leaves, dies or retires to be replaced by someone else, you cannot leave the personality of a business to fend for itself. It would be cacophonous, inconsistent and discontinuous. The personality of a business can only be and must be man-made. Any change in that personality, likewise, has to be deliberately made.

Nor is the shaping or changing of a corporate personality something which can be confined to the boardroom or to the public relations department. A company's personality emerges from the cleaner talking to his mates in the pub after work just as it does from a TV advertisement, the annual report, a press release from the chairman, the conduct of a recruitment interview, the appearance and behaviour of a doorman, or a salesman's reference to a competitor's action. All those people represent the company. The company is everybody in it.

You cannot have a plush showroom for your products and a dirty, sloppy service mechanic to install them. You cannot authorize a backhander to a key customer and require an assistant buyer to return the case of wine a supplier sent him for Christmas. You cannot have pleasant, well informed people in your sales department and monosyllabic morons in your telephone exchange. You cannot report the success of your new product to shareholders if the factory is unable to cope with the massive returns of faulty goods. You cannot be moralistic and refuse to make an 'introductory payment' to an African official and expect the MD's secretary to book three flights, of which one will be used and none cancelled.

It is no coincidence that ethical considerations predominate in the examples given. Stakeholders will form judgements on a company's ethics first and consider those the most important. For two reasons it seems a good idea to set ethical standards at a high level. The first and obvious reason is that most stakeholders most of the time will appreciate a high ethical standard of behaviour. The second reason is that it is much easier to set and police high standards than low, dubious or uncertain ones.

On a rather lower plane, but still very relevant to people dealing with people, especially in marketing, is sincerity. Whitewash, paint over cracks and hot air do not belong in a well managed business. To talk about 'top quality' for a product that isn't, to say 'no artificial colouring' but keep quiet about all the fat and sugar, to send 'our furnishings consultant' when you mean our curtain salesman, or to call the business Kitchen Design Centre when it sells prefabricated kitchen units is insincere. Customers will find out without fail. Insincerity does not make and hold customers, and has an even more serious and demoralizing effect on salesmen. Yet it continues to be doled out every time that managing directors, amid the burlesque of sales meetings, ramble on about 'pride in our product' and fail to organize the continuous flow of very detailed knowledge with which every salesman should be crammed. They need complete, objective, quantified and demonstrable information on every aspect of the product offering of every competitor set against similar knowledge about the corresponding aspect of the company's own product offering.

CHANGE

There is a whole chapter (11) about change in this book. In it and elsewhere (Chapter 8) the quite dramatic changes in the behaviour and attitudes of consumers are discussed. It is noted how consumers are enjoying sharply increased standards of living and have become better informed, and how these circumstances have contributed to people's increasing independence and inquisitiveness. People have become self-assertive, sceptical, and vociferous, less prepared to accept authority and no longer interested in emulating the Joneses next door.

All that applies to consumers. Curiously, however, similar changes have taken place among the people who come to apply for jobs. In fact people have changed, full stop.

People's attitudes and behaviour change irrespective of the roles they happen to be cast in at any given moment in time. Attitudes and behaviour of people have changed and will continue to change whether they are customers, churchgoers, shareholders, lovers, holidaymakers, taxpayers – even when they are employees. Employees work differently from the way they used to, they communicate differently, they have different aims and they are motivated differently. This means that people should be recruited differently and their work organized and managed differently. Chapter 7 goes into that aspect.

GROWTH

I have yet to hear of a satisfactory, long-term way of keeping a business healthy without growth. Growth is a condition for survival, and managers have to ensure that the business grows because every category of stakeholder in the business expects growth.

One of the ways of providing 'growth' for a company is by buying or merging with another. Not infrequently this route is forcefully advocated by a company's chief executive whose personal ambition makes him want to run a bigger company. The gyrations in stock-market share prices (which come about largely through influences from outside the company) are then utilized to put together a deal which the shareholders of the target company find it hard to resist and those in the acquiring company impossible to prevent. In the ensuing annual report the Board proudly chest-beats about the 'growth' it has brought about. Well, real organic growth may ensue, but it may not – there are few areas of managerial endeavour in which more and bigger blunders are made than in acquisitions and mergers. But the actual deal brings no growth whatsoever. Sometimes some money changes hands, but much more often new pieces of paper are printed and swapped for the pieces of paper people already had.

In 1986 mergers and acquisitions in the United Kingdom took place to an aggregate market value of £13,500 million, £11,100 million of which was satisfied by printing and swapping bits of paper.* The stock market, in deference to the unreasonable belief that bigger is better, may award some growth in the market value of the new combine, but there is no growth in sales, profits, jobs, skills or customer loyalty. Growth, real growth that is, can only come from the people in the newly combined businesses, and then only if not too many of them have been antagonized, if there are enough with managerial ability and if any restructuring is always based on a profound knowledge of every aspect of the new combine. Since the ability to bring about an acquisition differs very markedly from the ability to run a much bigger and different business, this is not always the case.

So gripping is the prospect of instant 'growth' brought about by mergers or acquisitions that alternative routes to growth are not often considered. The reason for the wail about mergers and acquisitions in this chapter is that one of the alternatives is growth through people.

Growth through the company's own people may not be as spectacular as major acquisitions but it does have some very important advantages. It means that its people grow with the business and that they can be hired, trained and groomed for growth. It means that when a man is being succeeded, he is succeeded by a man capable of holding down a bigger job. Companies which grow mainly 'organically' can be, and tend to be, companies with sound human relations.

INVESTMENT

Not a government comes to power, not a captain of industry gives a speech and not an economist writes an article without talk of investment. 'The need for more investment in industry' as a cure for the country's industrial ills is an immensely popular scapegoat. What that

* The Stock Exchange.

additional investment should be in is not generally exposed beyond the knock-down expression 'in industry'. One thinks of machinery, buildings, computers and of course stocks and debtors. There appears to be a widely held belief that industry is a slot machine: you pop in your investment money and out come the profits. In fact industry is often more like a public telephone: you put in your money and absolutely nothing happens at all.

The idea of investing in people, by hiring and paying for the bright, energetic and imaginative ones to replace the nine-to-fivers and the Poor Old Freds, by training and educating them, by enabling them to acquire new skills and knowledge, and by briefing them and getting their commitment to the future of the company, are forms of investment which do not come in for a great deal of attention.

HOW MANY MARKETING PEOPLE?

I was visiting Charles Lubin, the founder and head of Sara Lee at the time when all the company did was to make the best cakes in the world. I asked him how many marketing people he had in the company. He replied: 'Let me see, we employ a total of 695 people; with me included that makes 696 people. Yes, we have 696 marketing people'.

In the culture of a company it is entirely logical and justified to put it about that it is everybody's job all the time to supply benefits to satisfy customers. Without satisfied customers there are no wages, no factories, no office, no raw materials and no lorries . . . and no business! Making people in the company aware of Charles Lubin's simple principle is vitally important, and it pays to do things which will acquaint people with customers and their concerns. Job rotation, project teams, plant visits from customers, product monitoring meetings with customers, awareness of the findings from research among customers, awareness of feedback from customers, and visits to customers are some of the things to which many in the company can be exposed. Leadership in this direction from the top down is an obvious way of stimulating this customer orientation. When he was executive chairman of General Foods, Charles Mortimer told me this:

> Most weekends I do the shopping for my wife, usually in a different supermarket each time. I look at our products and our competitors';
> I talk to hundreds of store managers and staff and to thousands of

shoppers. The value lies in the questions I am able to ask – from just about everybody – when I get back to the office on Mondays: it keeps our people on their toes and geared to customers.

The kind of customer orientation to which these comments refer is at the root of marketing because it implies that marketing is not just a cluster of managerial functions but rather a state of mind deliberately fostered among all who work in the organization.

CUSTOMER COMPLAINTS

It may seem like spoiling the fun to end this 'people' chapter with so sad a subject as complaints. Moreover, what have defective products got to do with people? Everything! Complaints are made by people about mistakes made by people which have to be set right by people to satisfy people.

Complaints shouldn't happen. But they do. Complaints arise for one of three reasons:

(a)   The supplier has done something wrong.

(b)   The customer is nasty or greedy.

(c)   There has been a misunderstanding between the supplier and the customer about what was to be delivered. Since the customer is right a priori, in most cases this is dealt with as a category (a) complaint.

Complaints from customers are obviously dealt with by someone in the marketing sphere; they are closest to customers. Let me submit a procedure:

All complaints are immediately fed to one man who must be given complete authority for dealing with them. This man I shall call S. O. Lution. Mr Lution acknowledges every complaint instantly. He is a senior marketing man who may be at director level. In his dealings with complaining customers he is identified by name and by title, which is 'director'. To the customer he is *the company*, not a department (not 'customer relations executive', certainly not 'complaints department'). He is perceived as a man who does not pass bucks. And he does not pass bucks.

Sol Lution's seniority has an obvious purpose within the company too. To fulfil his task, as will be shown below, he will have to bypass managers, upset procedures, rearrange priorities, interfere with work schedules and countermand people's bosses. Doing all these dreadful things, he will have to be obeyed implicitly. Such an improbable (and very necessary) state of affairs can be achieved only if Lution's managerial abilities are considerable and his managerial status unquestioned.

This is what Mr Lution does. Having acknowledged receipt of the complaint, saying, without any further commitment, 'You'll hear from me soon', he establishes whether it is an (a) category case or a (b) category case. A (b) category case he deals with himself, firmly, truthfully, tactfully and immediately. (This man Lution is quite a guy!) Of an (a) category case, he establishes precisely by whom the mistake was made. He then shoots the complaint straight down to that man, not to his boss, his team, his foreman or his patron saint. Mr Lution will then require the culprit to do two things, and to do them in a specified and extremely short space of time:

1. To provide him (Lution) with a sound, workmanlike excuse about why the mistake was made.

2. To send a copy of this to his immediate boss together with any additional comments, requests or suggestions for remedial action he wishes to make and asking his boss to take the matter up with Mr Lution.

The culprit's boss then gets in touch with Sol Lution. If he doesn't very quickly Lution will be on to him. S.L. is nobody's fool! If the culprit hasn't alerted his boss, he is in trouble and knows it. Mr Lution and the boss then agree on an outline remedial procedure. There may be fundamental ways in which the company mismanages its business. In that case Lution may have to move up the hierarchy to get remedial action at the level empowered to take it. Whether it is directly from the culprit's immediate boss or up through the hierarchy, Sol Lution is made quickly and fully aware of the remedial and/or preventative action taken. At this point contact between the culprit, the culprit's boss and Lution is re-established and the culprit's role analysed and assessed. At that time it is most helpful if the man in question could be (1) required to put things right (repair the defective model, go and apologize, produce a replacement, help out the customer, subsidized by his company – all these things whilst least disturbing the performance his job requires of him); (2) fired, if it is quite obvious that he has

been behaving irresponsibly, or (3) promoted or given more money if
it turns out that the man has been trying hard to get stupid procedures
in the company altered, and this complaint has finally brought the
thing to the boil.

This procedure has as its primary aims:

1. To reduce complaints and any symptomatic causes.

2. To vest, in one man, complaints, their causes and the action to
cure and/or prevent them. Many companies, because they divorce
these three elements, take years to rectify basic flaws in their procedures or management practices, and some never discover those
flaws. Vesting these responsibilities in one man means that the causal
links between complaints, their causes and their remedies are consistently linked not only to each other but also to time. Thus the
effectiveness (or otherwise) of remedial action is quickly established
and any significance in the location or causes for complaints quickly
emerges.

3. To vest, in one man, the authority to break through (any) organ-
izational fences, hurdles, and barrage balloons for the sake of a cause
which is so obviously a deserving one helps to underscore the importance of people's individual responsibilities towards the achievement
of the aims of the organization of which they are part.

QUESTIONS

1. How has your Company organized its relationships with its
   various groups of stakeholders? Is there someone responsible for
   the relationship with every one of those groups or are any
   ignored?

2. What do you know (not what do you believe) about the
   perception of your Company among the various groups of
   stakeholders? Does a consistent 'personality' emerge? Is that the
   personality your Company is striving to create?

3. How does your Company think about growth? Does the Company
   seek to achieve at least part of its growth by organic means? If
   so, how does that aim translate into the way you recruit, select,
   educate, train, motivate and plot the careers of the people in your
   Company?

4

The Marketing Mix

Kissing don't last: cookery do!

George Meredith: *The Ordeal of Richard Feverel*

WHAT PEOPLE DO

Having considered some of the elements in the makeup of those fascinating creatures called people, let us consider in this chapter what they actually do in marketing.

TO HAVE YOUR CAKE

No word so aptly describes the essence of marketing as 'mix'. A mix is a composition of ingredients put together and processed in order to fulfil a particular purpose. Every ingredient in the mix matters, as do the amount and the precise attributes of each one. No single ingredient, nor indeed an incomplete mix, is capable of fulfilling or even approaching the fulfilment of the whole. Each ingredient depends totally on each and every one of the others for its contribution to the fulfilment of a purpose. Consider an analogy: raw eggs, sugar, rind of lemon, vanilla, butter or flour are not especially palatable on their own, but, mixed in the right proportion and properly processed, they can result in a cake tasty enough to satisfy the most spoilt of gourmets.

Just as there are endless varieties of cake made to suit different sorts of people with different means and differing tastes, in different countries and on different occasions, so there are an infinite number of marketing mix configurations. The mix in each case – and this is the essential part! – is composed for a specific purpose. The purpose is what

[33]

customers perceive as a value or a benefit, for which they are prepared to part with some of their money.

PRACTICE AND CONCEPT

As is the case with some other concepts in marketing, the practice preceded the formulation of the concept by many decades. The conscious juxtapositioning of product formulation, packaging, pricing, selling, distribution and advertising, and the adjusting of the relevant weight given to each in the light of the general effectiveness obtained, was common practice in the nineteenth century and, for all I know, before. The term Marketing Mix was invented by Professor Neil Borden in 1964. At that time, in America, it was very fashionable to try and reduce marketing to a state of science, and the marketing mix, in consequence, was dressed up with considerable complexity. The concept is too valuable to deserve that kind of treatment, and so I prefer to pass on the description in the *Macmillan Dictionary of Marketing and Advertising*, edited by Professor Michael J. Baker, which (in 1984) says:

> The marketing mix refers to the appointment of effort, the combination, the design and the integration of the elements of marketing into a programme or mix which, on the basis of the appraisal of the market forces, will best achieve the objectives of an enterprise at a given time.

Before we leave Professor Borden, let me give his list of marketing mix elements:

The Elements in the Marketing Mix
as perceived by Neil H. Borden

(a) Product planning (in manufacturing companies) and merchandising (a term used by Borden and others for the composition of a retailer's product range).

(b) Pricing.

(c) Branding.

(d) Channels of distribution.

(e) Personal selling.

(f)   Advertising.

(g)   Promotion.

(h)   Packaging.

(i)   Display.

(j)   Servicing.

(k)   Physical handling.

(l)   Fact-finding and analysis.

In the years up to 1929(!) Professor Borden, with the Harvard Bureau of Business Research, had been engaged in a survey to establish the extent of common rates of expenditure on the various marketing functions among wholesale and retail companies. Quite substantial similarities were found to occur. So when, in 1929, a similar study was conducted among food-manufacturing companies, it was anticipated that further similarities would be uncovered. They weren't. Borden said:

> The ratios of sales (revenues) devoted to various functions of marketing such as advertising, personal selling, packaging, and so on, were found to be widely divergent, no matter how we grouped our respondents. Each respondent gave data that tended to uniqueness.

When you read this, please remember that Borden was talking only about money. On the grounds of amounts of money spent Borden detected an element of 'uniqueness' among the competing firms in the food business at the time. When you think about how those monies were spent – in product composition, pack types, sizes and design, product ranges, pricing and discount practices, and all the other marketing mix elements – the 'uniqueness' of every single contestant in that marketplace must have been very pronounced indeed.

I mention Borden's 1929 survey for two reasons:

1. It may make us consider whether since 1929, in business generally, we have worked towards becoming more unique as individual companies or less so, and in either case why.

2. It will remind us of the immense scope which the thoughtful, conscientious and imaginative marketer has for bringing about uniqueness in the marketplace.

About what happened after 1929, we can only guess (Professor Borden did no further surveys). If Borden's observations of the food business had any validity for manufacturing industry generally, it would be my guess that uniqueness became relatively less of an asset during the 40 subsequent years when mass markets developed as people became more affluent and manufacturing and distribution technology more efficient.

The 1970s began to show the slow, certain and quite cheerful death of the mass consumer, and by the late 1980s any manufacturing company which is uncertain about the quantitative (money) or qualitative uniqueness of its marketing mix is in trouble (assuming it is still in business).

A SLIGHTLY DIFFERENT RECIPE

With the advantage of a quarter of a century of painfully sluggish thought on my own part and the most dramatic, lively and unexpected action brought about by the millions who make up the marketplace, I gravitate to my own description of the marketing mix. But before holding forth on that subject, let me say that, as usual, definitions do not matter all that much. It is the thought that counts. There is no need, for instance, to feel uncomfortable (or out of date) with McCarty's 4 Ps: Product, Price, Place, Promotion. It is the way that you fill out each of the Ps which determines whether, in a marketing organization, you are doing a marketing job.

The ingredients of the marketing mix are presented below. These headings have been chosen to reflect two circumstances: (1) that it is these elements which, properly conceived, weighted and co-ordinated, constitute the manifestation of marketing, for all of them are parts of marketing perceivable in the marketplace; (2) each of these elements forms a distinct functional area requiring not just specific funds, but specific skills, know-how, tools and management.

The Marketing Mix Ingredients

1. Product architecture.
2. Product-range planning.
3. Packaging.
4. Branding.

5. Pricing.
6. Distribution channel choice.
7. Selling.
8. Advertising.
9. Sales promotion.
10. Merchandising.
11. Distribution logistics.
12. Customer servicing.
13. Public relations.

So I end up with one more than the already exuberant Professor Borden (see p. 34). Moreover, I leave out two of his twelve.

About the first of Professor Borden's twelve I miss out, we can be brief. What he calls 'display' comes close to what I call merchandising. (What he calls 'merchandising' is included in my product-range planning.) The other of my omissions from Borden's list is more fundamental. Borden includes 'Fact-finding and analysis' as an ingredient in the marketing mix. I don't. I exclude it, firstly because fact-finding and analysis (very much marketing men's activities) are not part of what marketing makes manifest in the marketplace. Secondly, and more importantly, 'fact-finding and analysis' are avoided because they are an intrinsic part of bringing about and ensuring the effectiveness of every one of the ingredients and of the mix. Including fact-finding and analysis in the marketing mix is a bit like including the whisk and the mixing bowl as ingredients in the recipe for a cake.

WHAT MIX MARKETING?

An earlier chapter in this book, 'How Far Does Marketing Go?' (Ch. 2), makes what to some readers will appear as excessive claims about the realms of management which should come under the influence of marketing in well managed companies. Not quite so contentious perhaps is the concise enumeration of the functional areas within the marketing mix which thereby move in the orbit of marketing management.

1. Product architecture

Making (manufacturing) the product is not a marketing responsibility, and neither is engineering (figuring out how to make it), procurement (buying it, or buying the bits and materials to make it from), manning (providing the people required to make the product) or finance (providing the money to invest in working capital to provide appropriate quantities of product at the appropriate time in the factory warehouse).

What the product is meant to do for the customer, how it does it, the precise specification for it, the tolerated variances from those specifications and the acceptable cost of providing it – subject to due negotiation – *are* the responsibilities of marketing. I call these the *product architecture*. The architecture stretches from the chosen raw materials going into the product to the product in use by the customer during the entire period he expects to use it. In retailing, these functions are rather less complex, and those responsible for marketing may actually do the procurement job. In manufacturing companies, during the course of shaping the architecture of a product offering, marketing people will need to lean heavily on the skills and knowledge of procurement – research, engineering and manufacturing people and designers with whom they will be in continuous discourse about trade-offs and in negotiation about alternatives. If and when a product or service (or, as is becoming increasingly the case, a product/service package) has been agreed upon, the specification of that product (including the colour, varieties, size, design, performance, durability and reliability incorporated in that specification) is the responsibility of marketing people, as is the cost at which it is to be supplied (which has nothing to do with the price at which it is to be sold).

Of all the marketing-mix ingredients, it is the product architecture which companies most often leave outside the marketing orbit. This is foolish for two reasons: firstly, because marketing has the responsibility for having and holding customers, so it is marketing people who are most concerned with and knowledgeable about the consumer needs a product is supposed to answer; secondly, because it obstructs the very desirable harmony and the synergy between the product and the other mix ingredients. To locate product architecture (or any other marketing-mix ingredient) outside the marketing responsibility is akin to performing a symphony with an orchestra whose wind section is located on a different stage in the same hall, under its own conductor, who can't read notes.

2. Product-range planning

The product *range* and how it is brought into being is a distinct function in the marketing mix which does not have a great deal to do with the architecture of individual products. The determination of the range of products a manufacturer decides to offer or a retailer decides to stock is based on a number of quite specific criteria. The first one is economic. A product range may be broadened in order to increase the rate of utilization of a sales force, manufacturing facilities or distribution facilities; or a product range may be reduced for economic reasons to reduce investment in stocks, to lower unit cost of production or to concentrate the investment in advertising.

A product range may be broadened for tactical reasons. It may be undertaken to force up the size of retail orders or to fill up retail selling space and block out competitors; or, in the case of retailers, to cash in on specific seasonal or local events or trends or to put up defences against specialist competitors.

A product range may be changed for strategic reasons. Examples include repositioning the product offering (making the range acceptable to a new group of customers among either consumers or the trade), and exploiting the franchise built with the original product (we are seeing cosmetics, house building and, more recently, sports car manufacturers branching out into an exotic array of technically unrelated items).

As the 'make' choice in make-or-buy decisions for manufacturers is becoming somewhat less automatic, we see the marketing-orientated question 'What more can we sell the customers we already have?' asked more often. It has led to petrol stations selling umbrellas, grocers roast chicken, banks holidays and garden centres ice cream. It is obvious that consumers benefit from the increased competition this trend provides, and it is gratifying to observe that consumers are showing little aversion to accepting widely differing products coming from the same source (like underpants and smoked salmon from MIGROS or chocolate bars and radar sets from Mars).

Devising a company's product range is a distinct and important management function within the marketing orbit. This is most clearly illustrated in retailing, where no product architecture exists at all but where product-range planning determines the commercial success of the enterprise and is largely responsible for the 'personality' of the store.

3. Package

The reasons why packaging is listed separately are that some products
are sold without packages (and in that case, this ingredient can be
omitted) and that when the product is packaged, the package fulfils
one or several quite distinct marketing roles. A package may aid the
application of the product (aerosol), it may explain the function and
usage of the product (pharmaceuticals), it may have after-use value
(storage jars), it may explain contents (canned goods), or it may
embellish the product to justify its price (cosmetics). The package may
fulfil a host of more subtle functions, such as endorsing the benefit
offered by the product (polish), drawing attention to the generosity of
the buyer (gift packs), or glorifying the economic status of the user
(shopping bags from certain retailers). (It is worth noting that the
shopping bag is in fact the package for a service!)

A note about the design aspect of packaging follows below (p. 41).
To the technical, physical and cost aspects of packaging much the same
applies as for product architecture: marketing is wholly responsible for
the specifications and functionality of packaging, but these can be
brought about only through close and intensive collaboration with
and extensive input from the procurement, engineering, distribution
and manufacturing experts in the company.

4. Branding

Branding would not need to be listed as a separate marketing-mix
ingredient if all brands were single-product brands and all products
single-brand products. In those cases what goes for the product goes
for the brand. There was a time, in the 1960s and 1970s, when single-
product brands were immensely popular and indeed there are still
many around. There are two good reasons why single-product brands
are likely to face declining popularity, why product strategies and
brand strategies will need to be plotted independently of one another
and why, consequently, it is justifiable to give branding its own place
on this list. The first reason is that average product lives are shortening.
It is clearly foolish to invest in a brand if the life of the only product sold
under it is threatened. The second reason is that marketing expenses,
especially on selling and advertising space, are increasing ahead of
inflation, and thus threshold amounts of investment in marketing are
mounting to such a level that few single products are able to support it.

It is therefore likely that we shall see increasing emphasis on the building and maintenance of umbrella brands, i.e. brands under which a whole range of products is sold and whereby individual products in that range can be adapted or replaced without detracting from the investment in or the franchise of the brand. Products sooner or later die – brands can live forever. It may be perfectly businesslike to consider investments in products on a short-term basis, especially in volatile market sectors. Investment in a brand, however, only makes sense if it is long-term and continuous. The criteria and procedures in planning the future of an umbrella brand are quite different from those which apply to individual products sold under that brand. If the two are mixed up, a serious error is committed.

An example will serve to illustrate this point. Many manufacturers are trying hard to strengthen the brands they own, and they complain, understandably, about the squeeze exerted on their net selling prices by the all-powerful multiple retailers whose business they cannot do without. Some of these manufacturers, in the interest of beefing up the financial performance of their *product*, accept orders for that product under multiple retailers' labels. The more shortsighted of these manufacturers, moreover, manufacture the products under retailers' labels to the same formulation as is used for the product sold under their own brand. Since the pricing structure allows the retailer to sell his private label at 20 per cent below the price of the manufacturer's brand, the effect on the business done under that brand is very detrimental. So here we see how there is a conflict of interests between a (short-term) product strategy and a (long-term) brand strategy. The two can be, and in an increasing number of cases are, quite distinct managerial entities, but one cannot be determined without the other and the longer-term one of the two must of necessity prevail.

When we discussed packaging as a separate marketing-mix ingredient, we pointed out that some companies supply products without packages, and it makes sense in those cases to be able to drop such ingredients from one's list. The same applies to branding. People selling bridges, wheat, funeral services or fresh spinach do not use brands (I am not saying they shouldn't) – they can drop branding from their list.

A word about design

An element which needs to be singled out for attention as regards product architecture, packaging, product-range planning and branding is design. Design is an *integral* part of each of these functions, and it is through design more than through anything else that the cohesion between these functions is demonstrated and the 'personality' of the product offering expressed. Design is not an add-on – an *integral* part cannot be. Design (and the designer) is necessary right from the conceptual stage of products, product ranges, brands and packs. Design as applied to these functions can greatly enhance their effectiveness. Design can be the single, dominating factor behind the success of brands or products in the marketplace. Olivetti's commercial success is largely based upon the importance the company has attached – consistently for decades – to design. The success of retailing companies like Ikea, Habitat and Laura Ashley has been largely built on design. Small brands like Winsor & Newton and Elsenham (Quality Foods) have used design as a fundamental constituent in their product and brand strategies.

For small companies and small brands it is usually not economically feasible to build their own in-house design capability. For bigger companies and bigger (consumer product) brands it is, and I am strongly biased in favour of developing such a capability in those cases. House designers have two advantages over outside designers: a profound intimacy with the market in which the company operates and consistency across products and over time. Both are conditions for the maximum long-term effectiveness of the considerable contribution which design makes to marketing.

5. Pricing

Price and cost are two entirely different things. Marketing people have the responsibility for accepting the cost of a given item after due negotiation with procurement, manufacturing and engineering people. They will have to re-negotiate whenever cost constituents change or their 'contract' with the other departments runs out. Price is also determined by marketing people, but it is determined as a result of communication with an entirely different group, i.e. customers. Cost arises from raw materials, wages and overheads; price arises from benefits delivered.

Price can only be determined if customers have been accurately identified and if, subsequently, those customers have been made fully conversant with the value on offer. Whether the necessary communication with customers takes the form of face to face negotiation (when selling a bridge or a ship), trial and error in a test market (when pricing a pack of breakfast cereals) or research (when introducing a new model of washing machine) in no way detracts from the circumstance that price can only be determined through the discovery of what customers perceive the value of what is offered to be. The precise pinpointing of customers is necessary because of the way customers' circumstances dictate both the values they are looking for and the prices they are willing to pay. The value of cool drinking water and the price chargeable for it in the heart of the Sahara is quite different from that which is appropriate for the Water Board in Limerick. If you are selling motor cars to millionaires, you will only make a sale if values far beyond mere personal transport are offered, but by doing so you can then price at five times as much as an ordinary car.

Price is more than a justifiable recompense for value delivered – in many instances price plays a communicative role. A price ending in . . 99 tells us 'this is cheap'. If two apparently comparable products are priced at 50p and £1, to some buyers that will suggest that the £1 product is of better quality, but to others it will suggest that the 50p item is better value for money.

The communicative role of price must also be considered in the marketing mix. Imagine producing well designed, good quality woollen carpets, sold through high-class outlets and advertised in glossy magazines. If those carpets were priced in the lower middle price range for carpets, the pricing would undermine the rest of the marketing mix; sales would be lost and brand and product image damaged. It is this communicative role of price which causes manufacturers to get angry when retailers use their brands as loss leaders.

Pricing can have tactical functions – apart from its use in straight price warring, offering products in a range of qualities/prices (price lining) is aimed at simultaneously locking out several competitors from retail shelves. Pricing can be used to change or broaden the group of customers the marketer wants to cater for, and to buy one's way into retail sectors not previously serviced.

Elsewhere it has been observed that products in markets can move readily downwards along the socio-economic ladder, but that moving up that ladder is tricky and time-consuming. Similarly price can be lowered much more readily than raised. For many products raising price is possible only to follow inflation. A price reduction therefore tends to be irreversible. Price often appears to be the most popular of marketing-mix ingredients and some of the reasons for this will be discussed later in this chapter. Here it is relevant to sound a warning about an old and still popular belief encouraged by economists and

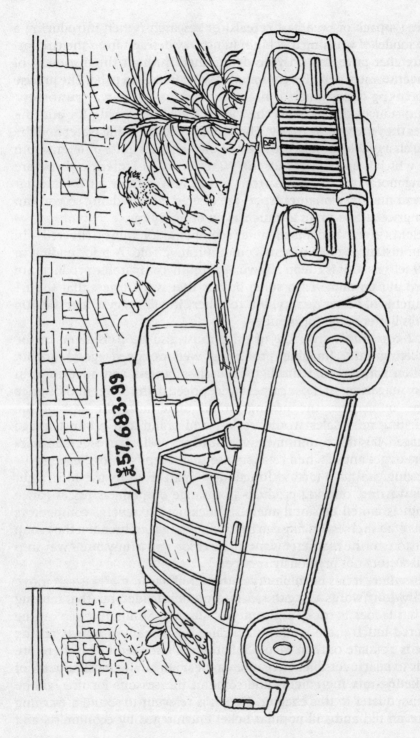

A price ending in . . . 99 tells us 'this is cheap'.

other worthies: if the price goes up, demand goes down, and if the price goes down, demand goes up. This is far too general and thoughtless an idea to hold any truth other than on an incidental basis. No marketer should ever contemplate any price changes merely on the basis of this flimsy idea.

6. Distribution channel choice

The choice of distribution channel may be dictated by circumstances. For example, a supplier entering a new market may decide to place his selling in the hands of a sole distributor or a broker; where his products are sold therefore depends on where the distributor or broker calls. Another supplier (good as his product may be) who is small and unable to fund heavy promotion investment may find himself locked out of the multiple chains and find his distribution confined to the independent retailers. One of the pillars upon which the birth of freezer centre retailing was based (see Chapter 11) was the circumstance that many medium-sized frozen-food suppliers were unable to find their way into the mainstream grocery trade. An obvious example is the retailer who supplies his own goods for sale under private label but finds it impossible to supply other retailers therewith, they being loath to buy from a competitor.

An extreme case of circumstance dictating the choice of distribution channel was the garden-tool manufacturer Wilkinson Sword, which pioneered the high quality stainless steel razor blade. Enthusiastic consumer response to its invention caused the company great embarrassment, because it had neither the manufacturing capacity nor the marketing wherewithal to meet the demand; and so, for a time, if you wanted Wilkinson blades, you had to buy them, one pack at a time, from hardware stores! Generally, being dictated to by circumstances will be the more prevalent the less (financially) powerful the supplier is, the less unique his product offering and the remoter his market from the main centre of his business activities.

But no marketer should ever relinquish all influence over where his products are sold, and a responsible marketer will ensure that he retains ultimate control over where his product is, and where it is not, made available for sale. The law in some countries requires a supplier to offer his goods to whichever retailer expresses a wish to buy them, and in others it is illegal to discriminate against retailers through differentials in prices and conditions. Much as such legislation may be perceived as a curtailment in the freedom to trade, such requirements have obviously to be adhered to. Even so, most suppliers have considerable discretion in choosing the distribution channel for their wares, and that choice should be based not only on the circumstances under which the supplier operates but also by the need for maximum compatibility with the other marketing-mix elements. Here again the type of outlet where a product is sold should reinforce the other marketing-mix factors, not undermine them. Since the retail scene in most developed countries is very dynamic, new opportunities frequently present themselves and frequent adaptations have to be made. If a company has made no significant changes in its distribution strategy during the past 5 years, chances are that it is missing opportunities or heading for problems. It took Birds Eye, Findus and Ross, which between them dominated the frozen foods retail market in the UK in 1969, years to respond to the emergence of the freezer centre mentioned above. By the time these companies took action it was too late for them to build anything but quite minor market shares in this distribution channel. Suppliers of confectionery and snacks who are not now supplying garden centres are missing substantial amounts of business.

Finally, under this heading, let me point to the very innovative thinking which some companies have applied to distribution channel selection. Smith Kendon was a retail chemist business which made medicated boiled sweets on a small scale. The company grew out of all recognition because it developed the idea of merchandising a range of candies in the service stations and restaurants along the motorways of Europe. Bo-frost and Eismann (for frozen food) in Germany and Davenport (for beer) in England decided they wouldn't use retailers at all and set up house-to-house distribution capabilities. Sometimes the initiatives for innovative distribution routes are taken by retailers themselves: retail banks now sell holidays, grocers sell banking services and superstores sell motor cars.

7. Selling

Selling is the sharp end of marketing. It is only through salesmen that a company can present itself face-to-face to its primary customers. Selling is an extraordinarily difficult job, and it is getting more difficult all the time, for two reasons. Firstly, the complexity of the retail trade is increasing fast as the traditional source-of-supply-based divisions between the retail trades is being replaced by a set of very large general retailers on the one hand and many new types of consumer-life-style-orientated specialists on the other. Secondly, retailers generally and large retailers especially have been hiring increasing numbers of highly skilled marketing specialists, in a dialogue with whom the traditional salesman will be instantly outwitted.

There are instances of well run manufacturing companies which, faced with a high degree of concentration among the retailers through which they sell, now deal with a much reduced number of retail accounts and now require a smaller sales force than before. Along with this legitimate slimming down of the sales force has come the slowly growing awareness of what marketing is and this has contributed to an attitude that marketing (i.e. advertising, sales promotion, merchandising, sales servicing) has to an extent *replaced* selling. This is dangerous nonsense. The need for aggressive professional selling is greater than ever. To provide the wherewithal with which to achieve professionalism and aggressiveness in selling has grown into an enormous, daunting and continuing task. Here is my analysis of where, in general, the greatest shortcomings in today's salesmanship lie:

1. Salesmen are not given credit for being capable of understanding that their company, and therefore they themselves, are in business to produce profit, not market shares or sales volumes.

2. Salesmen are not treated as integral members of the company. Salesmen should know their way around the company. They must be severely taken to task for committing the company to what it cannot do and, conversely, those in the company responsible for failing to carry out what salesmen have reasonably committed the company to do must be rooted out and dealt with.

3. The communicative skills of salesmen are not assiduously developed and trained to respond to the much increased sophistication of the buyers they are meeting with.

4. The knowledgeability of salesmen is inadequate. Profound and up-to-date knowledge is now an absolute condition for any attempt at successful selling. Training standards should aim at providing salesmen with more knowledge about the customers' business environment than the buyers they encounter possess. (If that sounds like a tall order, it can still be met.) That knowledge should include detailed insight into the activities of the salesmen's competitors.

8. Advertising

The place of advertising in the marketing-mix is obvious when we consider that it is chosen to do communication and/or selling jobs when the desired effect from it can be achieved more cheaply than by other means. Not all commercially generated advertising sells and not all advertising is intended to sell. Advertising may be used to inform a million housewives that the refurbished Bloggs and Son store opens next Tuesday or that those wanting to test drive the new V-16 Mercedes-Romeo should fill in and mail the coupon below. Advertising may not even mention the product and merely splash out the name of the supplier or the brand ('The Chase Manhattan Bank' or 'Dubonnet').

In all cases, and certainly if advertising does have to sell, it is wise to determine what its effect is required to be and what it is likely to cost *before* the investment is made. A required effect might be: 'to acquaint the 55,000 households who will be buying a new washing machine with the attributes and the price of our new model', 'to obtain 15,000 orders for our pack of mixed flower bulbs' or 'to ensure that 260,000 new car-buyers are made aware of our company's nomination for the Best Car Service of the Year Award'. Research people and media experts will then have to estimate the exposure required to obtain the desired effect and calculate what the cost of doing so would be. Several alternative marketing mixes will then be tested to ascertain whether it is the intended use of advertising which is the most cost-effective way of going about it.

Advertising more than any other part of the marketing mix suffers from the difficulty of measuring its effectiveness (let alone predicting its effectiveness before it has happened!). That effectiveness is determined by the amount of it (inches, seconds, pages, frequency), who are exposed to it (media selection) and what the audience is exposed to (message). Especially if there are precedents or sound research data, density of exposure of media effectiveness can usually be predicted with some measure of reliability. When it comes to assessing the effectiveness of alternative 'messages' – the qualitative aspect of advertising – we are in a nebulous area. There the man fighting for an advertising budget is at a disadvantage against those advocating a sales-promotion campaign or a price cut.

It is too seldom realized – in the heat of finalizing next year's marketing plan, say – that advertising can undermine the long-term health of a product or brand only through blatant stupidity, and that it is entirely reasonable to expect advertising to enhance the image and the long-term health of a brand or a product. Price-cutting exercises and some forms of sales promotion, effective as they may be predicted to be in the short term, are quite dangerous drugs where the long-term health of products or brands is concerned.

The practice of advertising seems to suggest that it is often executed in isolation – that it is not truly blended into the marketing mix and that, thereby, opportunities are lost for product, pack, price, selling, and merchandising to strengthen and to be strengthened by branding and advertising.

9. Sales promotion

Sales promotion is *temporarily* offering customers more than normal with the specific purpose of *inviting trial* of the product concerned. The customers in question may be the trade or individuals or both. Although not usually called by that name, sales-promotion tactics are used in industrial markets, as when reduced prices for trial orders are granted. The vital difference between sales promotion and bribery is that bribes are offered and taken in secret, whereas sales-promotion offers are there for all to see and respond to.

The strengths of sales promotion are its immediate effect and the controllability of its cost. (Using marginal costing, the risk of losing money can be eliminated and the sales-promotion programme can be self-liquidating.) The crucial point about a sales-promotion pro-gramme is to ensure that it does benefit new users only, and that it does not subsidize buyers who are already customers. In the case of trade promotions this is no problem, not at least when customers are approached individually – except in countries where price discrimi-nation between customers is illegal. For consumer products to limit the sales promotional offer to non-users is usually impossible, and the marketer is reduced to choosing a communications mix biased towards the profile closest to that of his non-users. There is one medium – direct mail – where it is sometimes possible to 'purge' the mailing lists, i.e. remove all those to whom one does not wish to make the offer. Subsidizing regular users is not only expensive and wasteful, it can have the additional negative effect of frustrating or irritating the customer. The man, for example, who has just paid a year's full subscription for a magazine will feel cheated on receiving the offer of a 30 per cent reduction in the subscription to that same magazine plus a pocket calculator and a special mid-year report if he fills out the coupon now.

It was stated earlier that a promotional offer is a temporary offer. There are a number of obvious reasons for this: if it doesn't work quickly, it is unlikely to work at all. As long as the duration of the promotion covers the buying cycle for the product category in question, the buying opportunity has been provided. If the costing of the promotion leaves the marketer out of pocket, then obviously the longer it lasts the more costly it becomes. But the most serious effect of over-extending a promotion programme is that it undermines the credibility (among consumers as well as the trade) of the regular value/price perception. This situation arises when supplier A announces a deal which provokes supplier B to match it with his. Whereupon A follows on with yet a further promotion. Very soon neither the trade nor consumers will any longer buy the product at 'regular' conditions – their buying follows deals across brands and what started as a promotion for one brand has become a price reduction for the entire product category. The less the differentiation between brands, the sooner this situation is reached. The only remedy is difficult and time-consuming, and lies in the skilful orchestration of the *other* marketing-mix elements.

10. Merchandising

Merchandising is the selection, combination, presentation of and provision of information about goods at the point of sale. Its purpose is to aid customers in the selection, combination and buying of goods. Merchandising is relevant in a wide variety of situations, from car showrooms to restaurants, from ships chandlers to drapery stores and from banks to garden centres. Merchandising requires skill, imagination and a profound understanding of the benefits of the product offering as perceived by customers.

The practice of merchandising is much more advanced in some countries than in others. Within Western Europe, Italy and the Benelux countries seem to lead the way; the British Isles and Spain are the least advanced. For small products with modest marketing budgets, merchandising (and store demonstrations or store sampling) is an economically feasible marketing-mix element when (national) advertising or promotion programmes are out of reach.

11. Distribution logistics

In this listing of marketing-mix elements, choosing the channels of distribution and getting the goods to the customers have been separated because they are two quite distinct things. True, the decision *where* to sell may be influenced by *whether and how* you are going to get the goods there. The aims of distribution logistics are cost-efficiency, reliability, punctuality and service to the customer. The choice of distribution channel is strategic: it is directly dependent upon the group of end-users the company wishes to attract and how it wishes to service them.

12. Customer servicing

The responsibility of marketing ends not with the delivery of the product, not with the payment for it, but with the consumption of the product or service that was delivered. In the case of an ice cream that may be 2 minutes after delivery, of a lathe 11 years, and of a life-insurance policy 6 decades. Marketing people sell benefits, not products, and so it is to the completed transfer of the benefit that the marketer's responsibility extends. It is this which distinguishes the marketer from the hit-and-run job lot trader. Marketing does not take on that responsibility out of pure magnanimity; it does so out of self-interest. Marketing is concerned with having and holding customers, not with bringing about one or more sales transactions. You can only have and hold customers if they are satisfied with the benefit you sold them. If they take a long time enjoying that benefit, the marketer has to be ready to service whatever it is he sold until the customer accepts that the product has finally done its job. For the marketer selling a good quality durable product the organization to service it quickly and effectively is vital to his own credibility as a supplier. The suppliers' most staunch and public supporters, inevitably, are customers who look after their purchase like an only child and make it last forever. To tell those customers 'Sorry, we cannot help you – the model you have is obsolete' is quite rightly taken as a personal affront, and anyone in the suppliers' company who dares to display such gross unperceptiveness should be severely taken to task.

The people a company uses to service customers are performing a marketing task, irrespective of whether they use pencils, screwdrivers, telephones or oscilloscopes to do the servicing. Before anything else,

these people must know that their job is to have and to hold customers
– just like everyone else in marketing.

13. Public relations

I am quite prepared to bow – halfway – to those who disagree with me
that public relations is a marketing function. Public relations is the job
of ensuring that all the representations made by anyone in the company to any of the company's publics, to any competitors or to any of
the media at any time are truthful, decent and supportive of the
company's policy. The tasks of marketing are directed at several of
these publics, and must take into account the needs and sensitivities of
all publics and rely heavily on communicative abilities and tools. There
are considerable overlaps and parallels between public relations and
marketing, and there are certainly PR tasks which are direct parts of
the marketing effort, and which therefore belong in the marketing mix
– just as salt does in the recipe of a cake, much as it may also have
useful roles in soups, salads or soufflés. Public-relations tasks in
marketing may arise from the need to brief prospective customers on
the worthiness of a company which, with a new product, wishes to be
considered as a supplier. A public-relations task arises from the need to
introduce the newly appointed managing director of an engineering
company to key customers. Public-relations skills and tools are needed
to brief the press when something in the company's advertising has
inadvertently upset a minority group among customers.

I am not too concerned about where in an organisation the PR
function is housed. I am concerned that public relations is a necessary
and valuable ingredient in the marketing mix and that it should be
capable of functioning in that context.

HARD AND SOFT

The marketing mix is the ideal home for a concept with a description of
which I want to close this chapter: it is the concept of the 'hard' and
'soft' constituents in the marketing mix. The distinction between hard
and soft constituents is extremely important in planning marketing,
and that distinction does not readily emerge from the listing of
elements discussed above.

The hard constituents of the marketing-mix elements are those whose effect is measurable and predictable and whose input is quantifiable and relatively large. Between them the hard constituents in the marketing mix make up the bulk of the marketing expenditure, and you can change that expenditure not by altering the nature of those constituents but by altering the amount you use of each. Money buys you a certain amount of a hard constituent, more money buys you more, less money buys you less. Salesmen's salaries, advertising space and delivery lorries are examples of 'hard' constituents. Price is often used as one.

Soft constituents of the marketing-mix elements are those which are qualitative in nature. The amount of money spent on them does not relate accurately to their effectiveness, and the aggregate amount spent on soft constituents is much smaller than what is spent on the hard constituents anyway. Soft constituents come about through the imagination, inventiveness, knowledgeability, intelligence and skilfulness of people. The effectiveness of soft constituents is far more difficult to predict than that for hard constituents. Even so, occasionally the effectiveness of a soft constituent reaches dizzy heights, far exceeding that of the hard constituent of the same element in the marketing mix. The product architecture of the Wilkinson Sword razor blade; the platform of the Doyle, Dane, Bernbach advertising campaign for Volkswagen; the selection of motorway service stations as outlets for Smith Kendon candies; and the merchandising units devised for Ferrero's Tic Tac are examples of daring and highly inventive soft marketing-mix constituents which have become classic successes. It is the soft rather than the hard constituents that contain the seeds from which the personality of the marketer's company and the image of his brand and product grow, and it is from those soft constituents that those products and brands are remembered . . . and bought again.

At the risk of over-simplification, I suggest in Table 4.1 how the elements in the marketing mix might be broken down into 'hard' and 'soft'. Some are all hard, some all soft, most a bit of both.

I have tried to point out, and Table 4.1 has attempted to summarize, the difference between the 'hard' and the 'soft' bits in the marketing mix, and I have suggested that the cost-and-effect relation of the 'hard' constituents is to some extent predictable, whereas the cost-and-effect relation of the 'soft' constituents is not – or very much less so. I have also given examples of where the cost-effectiveness of 'soft' constituents has been so effective as to make any comparisons with 'hard'

TABLE 4.1 **The marketing mix dissected**

Hard	Element	Soft
Formulation Tolerances Costing	Product architecture	User perceptions Design
Materials Varieties	Packaging	Application Psychological attributes Design
Economics Make-or-buy	Product range	Strategic/tactical functions Design
Support requirements	Branding	User segmentation Long-term considerations Design
Money	Pricing	Value Strategic/tactical considerations
Logistics	Distribution	Channel selection
Salaries/expenses (Staffing)	Selling	Education/suport Briefing/training
Space/time frequency	Advertising	'Message' Design Media selection
Duration 'Weight'	Sales promotion	Targeting Design of programmes
Staffing	Merchandising	Design Briefing/training
Tools Staffing Procedures	Customer servicing	Customer relations Consumer loyalty programmes
Staffing Co-ordination	Public relations	Co-ordination with marketing Pro-active Programmes

laughable. Given that the cost of the soft ingredients is usually much lower than that of the 'hard' ingredients, any marketer worth his onions would milk the soft ingredients dry before administering the hard. Most marketers don't. Why not?

1. Because they have not thought through that there is a distinction between hard and soft and what that distinction implies.

2. Because the attributes (imagination, inventiveness, originality and profound knowledgeability) with which to devise ultra effective 'soft' ideas are scarce.

3. Because bosses live in a different world.

Upon 1, I hope the above may shed some light. Of 2, I can only say 'Yes, but keep trying'. About 3, bosses prefer the devil they know to the devil they don't.

Managers prefer to authorize spending £400,000 on the kind of sales promotion campaign that worked so well 18 months ago than £40,000 on an assignment to a design house of which they have never heard. Bosses feel much more comfortable listening to a sales manager who predicts that a 3 per cent extra discount to the trade will yield extra sales of £4 million, than they will feel listening to a product development manager who has proposed to hire and equip a very bright technologist at a cost of £100,000.

Bosses will opt for the calculated over the incalulable, for the predicted over the unpredictable, for the accurate over the estimated and for the quantitatively argued over the qualitatively argued. In fact they will choose the hard over the soft.

That is why the marketplace is full of boring, half-dead, 'hard' marketing and desperately short of imaginative, enticing, audacious, innovative, daring, creative and dynamic manifestations of the worthy art of marketing. That also is why capable and imaginative marketing people have the most enormous, tough and challenging of jobs in business . . . they have to sell not just to customers, but to bosses.

Have another look at Table 4.1. You would think that it makes sense for companies to develop their capabilities in the soft areas, since they can be so very cost-effective and since they are largely responsible for corporate, brand and product 'personalities' as they are perceived by the company's various publics, especially customers. But most companies do the opposite: they will hire a PR officer, but use a PR agency for ideas; they will have an advertising department, but get not just the ads but even the ad strategy from their agency's creative people. Companies will insist on investing millions in a factory full of manufacturing equipment, but they go to a product-development agency to help figure out what that factory will be producing. They will hire dozens of salesmen and buy cars for each of them, but they will rely on sales trainers from outside to teach them to sell. They will spend millions on packaging materials and machinery, but go to a design house (or, much worse, their printers) to work out what the packs will look like. Isn't that rather silly?

REACTIVE?

The stance taken in this chapter is deliberately *pro-active* (you initiate in order to make things happen). But it would be unreal to suppose that *reactive* use of the marketing mix (you do something in response to something a competitor has done) can be ruled out. There are two 'rules' with regard to such responses I strongly suggest marketers adopt:

1. You avoid tit-for-tat responses, i.e. you don't respond to a pack redesign with a pack redesign, you don't respond to a trade promotion with a trade promotion and, most important of all, you don't respond to a price cut with a price cut! Rather you rustle up all the inventiveness you can muster and let it loose on the other twelve marketing-mix ingredients.

2. You pull out all the stops on your 'soft' ingredients before tackling the 'hard' ones. It is cheaper and it can be more effective.

TIME AND TIMING

Just as time and timing are crucial in cooking, so they are in working with the marketing mix. In industrial marketing the amount of time which elapses between making an offer to a customer and obtaining an order (proof, that is, that the marketing mix was effective) may be a few days. In the case of consumer goods it may be several years. For each type of product offering an estimate of the time required to obtain consistent market feedback must be made, because that is how long the launch programme must be run. It also determines the amount of marketing money the company must be prepared to put at risk.

Timing is a quite different and even more important element in

working with the marketing mix. Soon after the very successful introduction of a new technology in a given market is unlikely to be the best
time to introduce a product based upon conventional technology
there. Any marketer keen to enter a highly volatile market (hula-
hoops, Rubik cubes or CB radio) had better get in near the start or not
at all. Sometimes specific geographic areas for specific market sectors
establish pioneer status, and so following such patterns can yield leads
for (imitative) innovations (excuse the *contradictio in terminis*) in other
markets. For initiatives in the design of women's clothing look to
France; furniture, Denmark; consumer optical products, Germany;
consumer electronics, Japan; vegetables, Holland; confectionery,
central Europe; and so on. If there is any company famous for the
thoroughness of its homework, it is Unilever; homework has become a
religion there. A few decades ago the company had witnessed the rapid
growth of fish fingers in North America. After much homework, the
company's UK subsidiary Birds Eye launched UK style fish fingers in
the UK and the product quickly became successful there too. Next stop
Holland. There the first launch failed. More homework, more tests.
Second launch. It failed. In something like a two-year period Iglo,
Unilever's Dutch frozen foods subsidiary, launched fish fingers (locally
known as *vissticks*) *three* times. The third time it worked. 'We did the
homework; but we got the timing wrong the first couple of times', the
company said.

WHAT USE THE MARKETING MIX?

So what can this marketing-mix concept do for us? It brings home the
following truisms:

1. There are a lot of ingredients in the marketing mix. None must
ever be forgotten because the most effective solution lies in the careful
consideration, juxtaposition and dosage of each. It is sound discipline
to ask a man who wants authority to put through a price cut why, in
each case, he has rejected using one (or more) of the other twelve
marketing-mix ingredients. It is also sound to assume, unless there is
rock-hard proof to the contrary, that a tit-for-tat response to a competitor's action will be counter-productive.

2. No two mixes, even between similar companies operating in the
same market, are ever the same. The merit of one's own mix should

never be judged against a competitor's, but only for its long-term effectiveness.

3. The effectiveness of the marketing mix as a whole must always exceed that of the sum of its constituent parts; if it doesn't, there is something badly wrong.

4. The ratio between the cost and the effectiveness of any one ingredient varies with changes in the dosage of that ingredient in the mix. Given that there are means (of varying accuracy) to measure that effectiveness, the ideal mix is where the effectiveness-to-cost ratio of every ingredient is at its maximum.

5. Changes in the marketing mix are not administered willy-nilly. Time and timing are crucial qualifications.

6. There are 'hard' and 'soft' constituents in the mix. It is worth concentrating resources on the 'soft' because of their high potential effectiveness.

7. The marketing-mix concept is a useful tool in briefing non-believers or ignoramuses on what marketing is about.

WHAT MIX WHERE?

The concept of the marketing mix knows no geographic frontiers. Geography will impose quite specific tasks upon the way the mix is applied. The chapter which follows considers the geographic aspects of marketing.

QUESTIONS

1. The marketing mix contains a rich variety of ingredients. Think back to the last time a competitor provoked you to take retaliatory action. Did you go the tit-for-tat route? Why? Did you check through all the marketing-mix alternatives?

2. Make an inventory of all the people who ever see or talk to customers – salesmen, drivers, service people, telephonists, your secretary, your ad agency staff, etc. Have they all been trained/

instructed/briefed/dressed for the job of talking to your
company's only source of revenue?

3. If bits of the marketing mix get taken out of your hands – like
    retailers selling under their (rather than your) brands, customers
    setting up their own distributive machinery, or customers getting
    you to supply in accordance with specifications emanating from
    their R&D – do you do the long-term arithmetic as well as the
    short-term?

4. Make a listing of the criteria, and the numbers, used in drawing
    up your advertising and your sales promotion plans for the period
    (year?) ahead. Is Peter robbing Paul? Are you happy about the
    year after next, and the year after that?

5

The World Is Our Market*

Are we not inclined to *sell* at home with all the undoubted skills which we
have and then forget all the rules and just *trade* abroad?

Miles Colebrook of J. Walter Thompson Company
at the 1986 Admap/Campaign Conference

WHERE? . . . EVERYWHERE!

This book talks about marketing, full stop. It does not discriminate on
the grounds of race, sex or colour, nor does it discriminate on the
grounds of geography.

There is no such thing as 'overseas', 'foreign' or 'export' marketing
in the eye of the beholder – the customer. The customer is at home.
There is no reason to make the customer consciously choose your
product because it is foreign unless the customer sees your country as
the ideal foreign source of your kind of product – like Scotland for
whisky, Japan for cameras or France for fine foods. Even then, though,
you are competing in what is the home market to those who matter
most, your customers.

Competition is international. There is not a market left in the free
world (there are not many in the totalitarian world either!) in which
there is not significant international competition in many or most
market sectors. In most western world markets the only sectors without foreign competition are drinking water (i.e. the variety only available from the tap) and funeral services. Education, banking, catering,
insurance and publishing, a few decades ago as purely national as you
could imagine, are now providing increasing foreign competition.
Some sectors are showing combined foreign-origin market shares in

* 'The World Is Our Market' is the motto of the Institute of Marketing.

excess of those held by home producers: cars, drink, domestic appliances or electronic equipment are examples. What this means is that just about every supplier (not in the drinking water or funeral services business) is experiencing foreign competition in his home market.

It is because of the preponderance of international competition irrespective of where we sell that I do not treat 'export marketing' as an add-on chapter in the back of the book. International marketing is an inescapable dimension in almost any marketing effort anywhere.

There is no reason why a (new) company's first market should be its home market. Indeed whole industries have been built to make products to sell deliberately in other countries. The famous Chinese porcelain was made for European markets. Sherry was made in Spain and port in Portugal for the British and other NW European markets. The phenomenon is centuries-old and has its basis in the availability of raw materials, skills (and modest labour costs) in one country and people able to pay for the product in another. The phenomenon is more prevalent today than ever before in history as developing countries realize that the only hope they have of raising their own standards of living is by manufacturing and exporting to the (relatively few) developed countries the products the people there want and can afford to buy.

Much is made of the need to concentrate one's overseas marketing effort in a few markets, and I agree with that cautionary advice – each new cultural and language area entered poses the need for specific resources. Since resources are always scarce, scattering them is a recipe for failure everywhere. However, it can make good marketing sense to enter into international operations in several markets concurrently. Alternative international marketing strategies will be discussed in the next chapter; suffice it here to say that the more specialized the product or the finer the target market segment, the more readily should a multi-country operation be considered.

WHAT CRITERIA?

There is a greater proportion of internationally orientated companies in small countries (Denmark, Holland, Belgium, Switzerland) than there is in big countries (USA, Japan, China, Germany, Britain). It is not, however, appropriate to suppose that it is any easier to build international business for a company from a small country than it is for one from a big country. A $200 million company in a big country is the same size as a $200 million company in a small country. The difference in the ratio of internationally operating companies between big countries and small countries arises from the circumstance that the $200 million company in the big country can usually attain its size within the confines of its home market, whereas the company from the small country will almost certainly have had to seek international markets to enable it to grow to $200 million.

$200 million = $200 million; 200 kilometers = 200 kilometers.

This observation, however, still leaves room for a popular and widely held belief among businessmen, especially in big countries, which needs to be vigorously contested. This is the belief that the building of business abroad should not be entered upon till a strong position on the home market has been built. This belief is entirely without foundation; it is, coincidentally, indicative of bad business judgement. Surely the primary tasks of a business are to survive, to be profitable and to grow. To accomplish those tasks, then, priority must be given to those markets that have the economic, social and political conditions under which those tasks may be most readily accomplished. It would be only by the purest coincidence that the home market would offer such conditions. Supposing strong domestic companies within a given industry in the US, Japan, Germany, Britain, France and Italy all held the belief which I am challenging, then the implication would be that each of those countries held the best potential for that industry!

Profit potential, plus economic, political and currency stability (the latter is not the same as stability in the pound sterling exchange rate!) and the promise of market growth are the primary criteria for the selection of markets. Size, distribution of population and quality of communications are the secondary criteria. Proximity to one's factory gate is a criterion which should be low on the list.

THREE PRINCIPLES

Any plan for the initiation of sales in another country must be based on the following three principles:

1. It is prudent to assume that all foreign markets differ radically and in every respect from the home market and from one another – until there is adequate proof to the contrary.

2. Building a market position in another country requires the same kind of resources, the same amount of effort and the same amount of time as building a position in the home market.

3. Building a market abroad does not start with making the first sale there but with carefully planned homework.

1. Foreign markets differ radically

Much as our world is internationalizing, different countries still have very different cultures and languages. What is acceptable to consumers in a given country is dictated not just by those consumers' aspirations and needs but also by the culture and language of their country. The more traditional the consumer behaviour pattern in relation to a given product category, the greater the weight of cultural and language aspects. Even if the language aspect appears to have no influence, the cultural differences between countries rule out the automatic assumption that what will sell in one will sell in another. If that were otherwise, Britain would be selling an awful lot more in North America. It is essential, when considering marketing in another country, to assume that no element in the marketing mix as it works in the home market will work in that other country until adequate investigation yields proof to the contrary. Adopting this assumption is a much safer, cheaper, and in the end quicker approach to international marketing than blundering into another country with a domestic product offering.

I was recently shown a pack design from a French meat-products company which intended to enter English-speaking markets. On the home market the product was sold as *paté paysan*. On the design it was called 'Pastry with Peasant'. The D. E. Williams Company of Ireland makes an excellent liqueur called Irish Mist. Keen to foster exports, the company took a stand in a German trade fair. The display aroused considerable amusement among the usually unsmiling German fairgoers. Germans can understand the word Irish – it is close to Irisch, which is German for Irish. Germans also understand the word Mist, which is German for manure.

2. Same amount of effort when building business abroad

Miles Colebrook, quoted at the beginning of this chapter and talking on the same occasion about British companies, said: 'There are many occasions when I have met UK division personnel alongside export division personnel and couldn't believe they worked for the same company'. Why this stepmotherly treatment of foreign markets? A common situation is the £50m company with an 85-strong sales force, an advertising budget of £3 million and a marketing research budget of £140,000 for the home market operation, which decides to start exporting. The company advertises for an 'export executive', saying that 'knowledge of a foreign language would be an advantage' and offers a salary equal to that of the area sales manager for S. Wales. The successful candidate will then be equipped with samples of the home-market product, a list of f.o.b. prices, photocopies of letters from seven overseas distributors 'who have written in' during the last 2 years and the address of the British consul in the foreign country. With that, the hapless export executive will be left to fend for himself. Of course he fails.

Is there one good reason why building business in one country should be significantly easier, require significantly different types of resources or could be accomplished significantly faster than building a similar volume of business in another? Would we consider using an Italian with little knowledge of English to sell to our engineering customers in Preston? Would we commission a designer in Austria to create packs destined for consumers in Cumbria? Would we expect to do any business with the buying office of a large multiple retail company in London if we were unable to offer any support in sales promotion, advertising, delivery logistics, merchandising or sales servicing, whilst quoting prices f.o.b. Rotterdam? The average UK company's answer to any of these questions would be 'no'. Yet in the fictitious but not wholly untypical example given above, the unfortunate 'export executive' is being put in just these kinds of situation.

In marketing abroad everything is different, but everything is the same. Foreign markets differ radically from the home market, but the kind of resources needed, the kind of procedures followed, the general magnitude of investment in people, skills, hardware, customers and promotion, and the kind of time-scale necessary are all comparable to what would be required for a first assault in the home market. There are no short-cuts. What appear as short-cuts turn out to be dead-ends or treacherous roads.

3. The start is not the first sale

The better known the company is, the more apparent short-cuts present themselves. Here are examples of just such short-cuts:

- Your trade association suggests you might care to take a stand at a trade fair in a country in which you have done no business before. You arrange for some hasty translating of brochures and you actually work out c.i.f. prices. Your product offering is still that which is good for the home market and your familiarity with the overseas country is still a perfect void.

- A charming and voluble man from a potential export market visits your head office with the aim of acquiring the sole agency for your products in his country. Had you known more about conditions in that country, you would have concluded that a network of five regional distributors would best suit your longer-term business aims. Meanwhile, however, you are stuck with the sole agent because the law of his country makes it practically impossible to take the agency from him inside 3 years.

- You receive a sizeable trial order from a leading supermarket chain in a foreign country in which your company has done no business before. A long time afterwards, meeting price resistance from various buyers as you are trying to build up your business in that country, you discover that the supermarket chain in question has undermined your present price credibility because it used your product as a loss leader at the time.

It is safer, less wasteful, infinitely more effective and in the end quicker to know where you want to go before starting on the journey. There is one optimal way of building a market position in a foreign country. That optimum will never be realized (no optimum ever is in marketing), but it makes obvious sense to attempt to approach that optimum. The only way to do it is through conscientious and imaginative homework. There is no way any business can be effective without considerable knowledge of the environment in which it operates. Some of that knowledge obviously is gained as the operation progresses, but some of that knowledge is essential *before* the operation is started – precisely to avoid some of the harmful blunders in my examples, and precisely in order to ensure a situation which is close to the optimum.

WHO TRANSLATES?

If only companies – what I mean of course is the individuals in them – could rid themselves of the obsessive fear which stops them 'going foreign', separate the need to grapple with market circumstances, culture, and language from the very real skills, know-how, determination and imagination which nearly every successful business has, and utilize the latter to conquer the former.

In practice there are many different way in which firms successfully run multi-country business, whether as global corporations, multinationals or export-orientated companies. It is clear that where there is a corporate headquarters in one country and foreign operations in various others, a translatory process has to take place somewhere between the twain. That process, incidentally, covers not only linguistic but also cultural, circumstantial, environmental and physical aspects of the differences between the areas concerned. I believe it to be to the benefit of any business if that translatory process takes place well away from the sharp end of the business, well away from the direct and personal communications between the company and its customers, suppliers, employees, trade, government, research universe and information sources. Table 5.1 shows the (simplified) relation between the linguistic/cultural side and level of managerial responsibility.

TABLE 5.1 Managerial linguistic/cultural involvement in marketing abroad

	General management at Head Office	International (export) management	Local management (selling, buying, hiring, manufacturing, researching)
Perfect knowledge of language (native speaker); part of culture			Marketing planning Implementation Tactics Monitoring
Good language skills; receptiveness to and some knowledge of cultural circumstances		Marketing strategy formulation Planning Development Performance-monitoring	
Few or no foreign language skills; receptiveness to but no knowledge of cultural differences	Formulation of – corporate objectives – policy – strategy		

QUESTIONS

1. Assess the extent of the foreign competition your own company meets in foreign markets and in the domestic market. What are the differences in your company's competitive positioning as between those markets?

2. If there are main markets in which your company does not (seriously) operate, list all the reasons why this is the case. Now split those reasons into two categories: the good, sound business reasons and the parochial, historic, superficial, or complacent reasons. Is there scope for any fresh initiatives?

3. Now list the good, sound business reasons why your company does (or will, or should) enter a market.

4. Given that you cannot take your product everywhere at once, how would you determine a short list of markets? Then, how would you allocate priorities to the markets in that list?

6

The Strategic Options For International Marketing

But Lord! to see the absurd nature of Englishmen that cannot forbear laughing and jeering at everything that looks strange.

Samuel Pepys: *Diary*, 27 November 1662

MARKETING STRATEGY ABROAD*

We have looked at criteria for foreign market selection, at the principles which should govern any foreign marketing effort and at the cultural and linguistic barriers which need to be negotiated. If markets can be selected by means of the appropriate criteria, if the principles are adhered to and if the cultural and linguistic barriers are surmounted, then success in foreign marketing is within reach and the real hazards of blundering across frontiers willy-nilly have been avoided. There is, however, a further piece of perspective an understanding of which, it is hoped, will enable the international marketer to be more sure-footed. It has to do with strategy.

When the practice of marketing in more than one country is examined, the curious conclusion can be drawn that as far as the product or the brand are concerned, there are only three strategies. To describe them, I use the phrases:

1. Shot-in-the-dark marketing.

2. (Phased) internationalizing.

3. Global marketing.

* The concepts discussed under this heading and some of the text are taken from an article by the author, 'Winging it in Foreign Markets', which appeared in the January–February 1987 issue of the *Harvard Business Review*.

[71]

The international marketer will need to know what the differences are between those three, where he stands, and where, in relation to those strategies, he wants to be.

In international marketing there are constraints and checkpoints for every element of the marketing mix as we move from one country to another. Constraints are more prevalent and more demanding for some elements in the 'mix' than for others. Constraints are the most prevalent and the most demanding for the product, and its architecture, which we want to take abroad. The effect of constraints on the brand, in its severity, closely follows that on products and so, under this heading, products and brands will be in the spotlight.

The term 'global marketing' has gained immense popularity among marketers in recent years.

GLOBAL MARKETING – ALL RIGHT FOR SOME

The term 'global marketing' was invented by Professor Theodore Levitt in an article for the *Harvard Business Review* of May–June 1983. The term was new but the practice of internationalizing products, brands, selling, and advertising – either separately or together – was not new. In some cases it was more than 100 years old. Brands like Johnnie Walker, Van Houten, Coca-Cola and Heineken have been international brands for many decades.

I am not going to try and distinguish between 'global' and 'international' marketing, not, that is, in terms of how many countries you have to sell in before you can claim to be global. The essence of what I think Levitt means by a 'global' strategy is that you aim to satisfy a clearly defined cluster of needs among a clearly identified segment of a market universe in a politically heterogenous geographic area whose size is limited only by your ability to service it. There *are* differences between international and global marketing, because international marketing accepts strategies which are differentiated by political boundaries and global marketing does not.

Within the marketing mix the product must be the most crucial element in determining whether or not a global marketing approach is tenable. The product must answer similar needs among similar market segments in different countries. This means that the perceived product attributes cannot vary from one country to another. It does not mean that minor product variations, to answer national differences in taste, cannot be made; the products sold under the brands I mentioned earlier all have such variations.

CONSTRAINTS UPON INTERNATIONALIZATION

Product development, but also subsequent elements in the marketing mix when undertaken for markets which transcend national frontiers, run into a whole host of constraints. The first and most obvious one is that people in different countries use different languages. Rules and regulations are another obvious constraint: in most countries you drive on the right but in some you drive on the left. Climate imposes obvious constraints and so do economic conditions, race, topography, political stability, and the occupations that people have. By far the most important source of constraints and the most difficult to measure is that of the cultural differences between people brought about by history, education, economics, the legal framework, and a host of other environmental influences.

Cultural differences between countries affect different markets in widely divergent ways. Few international adaptations will be necessary for the man selling pocket calculators, credit card facilities or lubricating oils. Research will show that rather more adjustments will be necessary for the man selling soap, gramophone records or sweets. The international convertibility of products (and services) varies enormously from one product category to another. I am intrigued by how relatively simple services like retailing and retail banking are slow to globalize, whereas certain internationally operating hotel chains have succeeded in so standardizing their product that, as long as you stay within the confines of the hotel, it is impossible to tell whether you are in Vancouver, Kuala Lumpur, Stockholm or Torremolinos.

If any lessons are to be learnt about international or global marketing, they are most likely to come from an examination of products which are known to possess a low degree of international convertibility than from those that are easily marketed across frontiers. Therefore, to get an insight into some of the constraints upon the internationalization of products I shall use examples from the international and global marketing of food and drink products, since I believe the constraints upon internationalizing or globalizing food or drink products are greater than in any other product field I can think of. It seems safe to assume that a food or drink product which sells successfully in one country will not sell in another unless research explicitly predicts otherwise.

Having said that the international convertibility – or, if you want a really ugly word, the globalizability! – of food products is low, I need to add that it is lower for some than for others.

THE MAIN CONSTRAINTS

The causes for the constraints upon the internationalization of foods and food-product concepts are twofold: one applies to food and very few other product categories; the other occurs in a wide range of product categories. Respectively, they are *recognizability* and the *age symptom*.

1. Recognizability

In contrast to most other consumer products, people are concerned to know what food products are made of. They need to be able to *recognize* the raw materials in what they eat and often as not they will want to know the processing method used. That recognizability is required in the appearance, the taste and, in most cases, the texture of foods. No such requirements are imposed by consumers when they buy durables (except, to some extent, textiles), personal-care products or household goods, for example. It is interesting to note that in personal-care products people have come to accept fragrances which are not only man-made but are made no longer even to resemble natural substances (and are sold under brand names which do not either: Poison, Je Reviens, Impulse, Imperial Leather, Fergie). In food engineering no such developments have met with consumer acceptance other than for soya-based ingredients, certain soft drinks and savoury snacks. This recognizability constraint means that products based on ingredients which are well known in one country but not in another cannot be sold in that country because the ingredients are not recognized. The recognizability requirement also means that the extent of engineering and processing which can be applied to foods is limited. Conversely, it means that extensive processing is more acceptable in a country where the product is not traditional than in a country where it is: the share of extracted (soluble) coffee in coffee-drinking countries like Germany,

France and Italy is low, but in non-coffee-drinking countries like the United Kingdom, Ireland and China it is high.

2. The age symptom

The second constraint upon the globalization of food (and many other) products is the age symptom. There is a negative correlation between the international marketability of products and the *length of time* during which usage habits for those products have prevailed in the target market. The older the usage behaviour to which a particular product responds, the more unlikely it is that an unfamiliar variant of that product will be acceptable to consumers. On the other hand, the more recent a usage pattern, the more likely it is that one and the same product will respond to that usage in different countries. This age of usage symptom I believe to be of prime importance in international product development programmes. The reason for the phenomenon is not mysterious. Products responding to old-established usage patterns came to market at a time when countries, and indeed regions, lived in relative isolation from one another. In modern times our international communications have proliferated – we look at each other daily on TV – and so our newly emerging usage patterns are converging, thereby enhancing the globalizability of the new products which respond to those patterns.

The age symptom does not just apply to food products, as the following examples show. Garden spades bought in Switzerland, England or Holland look quite different from each other, but gardeners in those countries use identical motor diggers. Men's formal clothing, even though it evolves slowly over time, is made in response to very long established usage habits. You do not need to be a tailor to tell a German, a Frenchman and a Briton apart by the suits or the shoes they wear. But with the recent emergence of casual clothing, everybody wears the same jeans, T-shirts and Adidas shoes. Globalizing of products has often come from the needs of new strata of customers or – it doesn't matter which way round you put it – new strata of customers have come along when suppliers produced low cost, universally available, integrated products. The traditional, destination-orientated, do-it-yourself holiday was only for the small number who could afford foreign travel. The all-in, mass-produced, package holiday is sold for its promise of sun, sea and sand at extremely low cost, and the destination has become a matter of total unconcern to the retail supplier and of relative indifference to the customer.

Now for a closer look at those product fields with very low levels of international convertibility. People have been eating for a very long time. Differences in climate, soil, topography, race, religion, migration and overseas trading links have brought about vast differences in food and drink buying and eating behaviour between countries.

Just how great these differences are can be illustrated by consumption figures for European countries (see Table 6.1).

TABLE 6.1   Selected foods in EEC markets, 1983–4
– kilos per head*

		Lowest		Highest
Cereals	Holland	62	Portugal	126
Potatoes	Italy	35	Ireland	125
Sugar	Italy	26	Denmark	40
Vegetables	Denmark	58	Italy	179
Meat	Portugal	57	France	104
Milk	Portugal	74	Ireland	192
Eggs	Portugal	5	Spain	18

*Eurostat.

As regards drinks, I have avoided extremes – rather I have taken pairs of neighbouring countries. See Table 6.2.

TABLE 6.2   Consumption in litres per head, 1983

Spirits	Spain	7.5	Portugal	2.0
Wines	France	85.0	Germany	26.5
Beers	Belgium	128.0	France	43.7

When you examine these consumption patterns in more detail, you further discover of course that each of those countries has its own range of spirits, wines and beers – totally unlike that of another country.

But even in food and drink there are differences in the length of time during which specific behaviour patterns have existed, and here again we see a very low level of international convertibility for old-established patterns and we can identify newly emerged patterns to which internationally marketed products are responding. See Table 6.3.

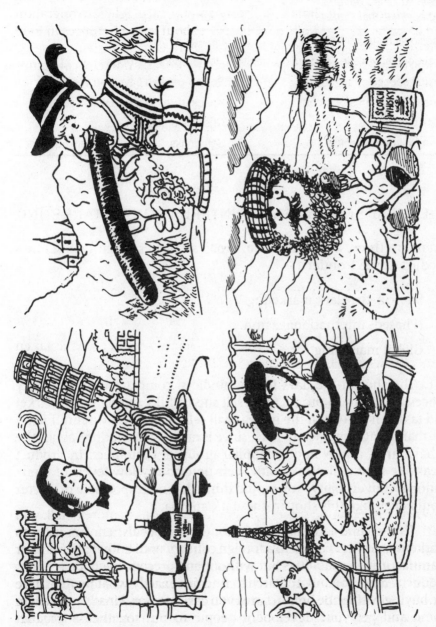

Just how great differences are . . . .

TABLE 6.3   **The age-of-usage-symptom for food products**

Old-established patterns (regional/national markets)	New patterns (globalizing markets)
Traditional restaurant menus	Fast-food menus
Most popular varieties and cuts of meat	Hamburgers, hot dogs
Natural cheese	Portion-packed flavoured yoghurt
Varieties and forms of bread	Knackerbrot, pizzas, Danish pastry
Block chocolate	Chocolate-coated bars
Beers, wines and spirits	Soft drinks, 'lite' beers, cream liqueurs

THE THREE STRATEGIES FOR INTERNATIONAL MARKETING

There are three, and only three, broad strategies when taking one's product across frontiers:

1.   Shot-in-the-dark marketing.

2.   (Phased) internationalizaton.

3.   Global marketing.

1. The shot-in-the-dark is the mindless, complacent, sloppy, lazy process of picking a product you sell successfully in the home market and taking it abroad in the hope it will sell there. It is by definition an un-marketing approach to take, since it makes assumptions about the behaviour of a new and unfamiliar group of customers. In product areas like food and drink, with their notoriously low levels of inter-national convertibility, you would think that no responsible marketer would ever take this shot-in-the-dark approach.

2. The second approach, by contrast, appeals enormously to marketing people: you go to a foreign country with knowledge of your manufacturing capabilities but without any preconceived ideas about products. Next you buy research to find out exactly what people there are buying within the product area you can cater for. Finally, you come home and get your developent people to put together a product offering with which you can compete in that foreign market. As I said, this is the approach we were all taught when we became marketing people.

3. The third approach is global marketing. Again this is a highly responsible approach from a marketing point of view. This time you go out into the world (well, perhaps you would go out into part of the world), ignoring frontiers, and you try to discover newly emerging needs to which, with your manufacturing capabilities, you might respond. You are particularly alert to consumer typology and to the behaviour patterns into which your product offering will have to fit. You do a very conscientious market segmentation job.

The global marketing approach is without a doubt the most worthy of the three: the approach promises you all the benefits from economies of scale without the concessions dictated by the need to maximize market penetration. You can afford to cream off your markets. You sell not what the greatest possible majority of consumers find acceptable but what a small minority of consumers are very keen on (a concept presented by Eric Morgan when CEO of British American Cosmetics). Let me give you some examples of products which were specifically developed to sell in global markets. Margarine was an early example, though it is curious that the originators of the product never adopted a global brand strategy for it. Schweppes Tonic, IDV's 'Bailey's Irish Cream', Ferrero's 'Tic Tac' and 'Rocher' are products conceived for global marketing. Other global brands, some with and some without global brand strategies, are Coca-Cola, Kelloggs, Heineken and McDonalds.

The phased internationalization approach – going into a foreign country and competing directly with the indigenous suppliers there – is exemplified by the Dutch selling Feta cheese in the Middle East, by the Danes selling British-style bacon in Britain or by the Swiss chocolate-makers carefully formulating their products to sell in American markets. Such brands as Heinz and such companies as Unilever have largely built their international business following this kind of approach. It has, however, a number of disadvantages:

1. First, a product specifically formulated for one particular foreign country, if it is in a low international convertibility category, is unlikely to be saleable in other countries. The Dutch do not sell their Feta cheese outside the Middle East, the Danes sell that type of bacon only in Britain, and the North American recipes of Swiss chocolate are unsuitable for other areas. As a consequence, following this strategy prescribes a country-by-country approach to international expansion.

2. Secondly, the foreign supplier in a market may have difficulty matching the value/price framework established by the indigenous suppliers with whom he competes.

3. Thirdly, the foreign suppliers may have great difficulty establishing their credibility. There are people producing a very good Camembert type cheese in Germany, but I imagine they would have problems selling their product to French consumers. Despite being the world's largest producers of Scotch-type whisky and producing an excellent product, the Japanese Suntory Company has thus far considered it unwise to sell its product in Britain.

The shot-in-the-dark strategy of selling abroad what you happen to be selling in your home market I have described as a mindless, complacent, sloppy, and lazy approach to international marketing. But wait . . . it is a strategy which has resulted in enormous export business all over the world. Practically all the world's wine-export business and the greater part of the exports of beers and spirits were built on this shot-in-the-dark basis. With 340,000 tons Holland is by far the largest exporter of cheese in the world, and nearly all of that volume comprises indigenous varieties. Germany has been building a very sizeable food and drink export business. It has done so mainly with unfamiliar, expensive, high quality products taken straight from its home market. And wait some more . . .

Earlier I mentioned Schweppes Tonic, 'Bailey's Irish Cream' liqueur and some Ferrero products as having been deliberately developed for a global market – and they were. I then mentioned Coca-Cola, Kelloggs, Heineken and McDonalds as other global brands, which they are – or, more strictly speaking, which they became. Those brands and products were *not* deliberately developed for global markets. They were developed, and for many years sold, only in their respective home markets. I am not suggesting that these products, once they had become established in their respective home markets, were taken to foreign markets willy-nilly. Extensive research, testing and reformulations have preceded the international roll-out of all these brands, but the origin of the product concepts sold under them was domestic, not international. It follows inescapably that the growth of these brands into global dimensions was based on a shot-in-the-dark strategy. And when you think about it, that applies to most global or international products or brands.

Let me illustrate this important point. The United Kingdom has a massive debit balance of trade where food is concerned. I made an estimate of the consumer value of products which had been *new* to the UK market during the past 20 years. That worked out at £3 billion, more than 10 per cent of total household spending on food. Apart from indicating that Britons are extremely innovative food consumers, I was further able to estimate that 85 per cent of those new products were either imported from or based on existing product concepts in other countries. As far as Britain is concerned, by far the most fruitful source of new food product ideas has been, and is likely to remain, existing products in other countries. You could extend the argument by predicting that of all the new products coming to the UK market during the remainder of this century, 85 per cent will have been on prior sale in some other country.

In nearly all cases these products have come to Britain on a shot-in-the-dark basis.

Although in theory the shot-in-the-dark strategy is wholly reprehensible, in practice it has proved to be the most significant; and the global marketing strategy, whilst in theory the most laudable, in practice has proved the most difficult to implement.

CONSEQUENCES FOR PRODUCT/MARKET STRATEGIES

What are the consequences of factors I have mentioned for international marketing strategies and for the knowledge, from research or otherwise, on which those strategies should be based?

1. First, the alternative generic strategies of global, phased internationalization and shot-in-the-dark must be assessed and choices made, since these choices will govern the entire product development process.

2. With knowledge of the technological resources available, target markets should be assessed, not only for size and growth rate but for the 'age-of-usage' and 'recognizability' characteristics I have mentioned. In a target market sector characterized by old-established usage habits, a product offering closely tailored to established product attribute expectations will be required and a country-by-country development route will have to be chosen; shot-in-the-dark or global approaches are unlikely to work. Conversely, if it is the ambition to

aspire after a global strategy, a geographically wide sweep will need to be made in order to ascertain whether any newly emerging need patterns are discovered to which the technological resources are capable of designing a response.

Whilst a shot-in-the-dark approach has a very good chance of failure, it may be developed as the basis for either a phased internationalization or a global strategy and it should certainly be tested against these possibilities.

3. As in the case of any marketing development programme, a stringent knowledge-gathering exercise will need to be mounted. The investment of resources in any serious attempt to expand sales abroad is considerable, and needs to be protected by appropriate knowledge. To acquire that knowledge, three types of inquiry are necessary:

(a) *Scanning*: the collection of data, trends, judgements and values which will affect, either directly or indirectly, any envisaged marketing operation.

(b) *Inferencing*: when a target group of customers responds in a particular way to influences in its environment, to speculate (and subsequently to test) about related responses to those same influences or about its responses to related influences.

(c) *Propositioning*: having assumed or ascertained a particular customer need, to propose a product offering in response to that need and measuring customers' assessment of that product offering.

From what I have said it will be clear that the emphasis in the case of a global aspiration will initially concentrate on scanning and inferencing types of inquiry. A phased internationalization approach will start with a scanning exercise, soon to be followed by propositioning type tests. The shot-in-the-dark approach will go straight to propositioning inquiries.

WHAT ABOUT BRANDS?

I suggested earlier that the product, of all the marketing mix elements, is the most restrictive when a global strategy is considered.

Some brands are linked with specific products, and what applies to

To propose a product offering.

the product applies to the brand. Coca-Cola and Kaffee HAG are examples. Other brands are associated with broad ranges of products: all private-label brands and brands like Hero or Kraft come in that category. In the former case the globalizability of the brand is confined to that of the product; in the latter the brand can be globalized to cover product ranges which are internationalized, i.e. product ranges are formulated to local needs, country-by-country. With regard to food and drink products, the opportunities for globalizing products are much more limited than the opportunities for globalizing brands, provided those brands leave a wide enough latitude to encompass product ranges formulated to suit the needs of individual markets.

SHOT-IN-THE-NOT-SO-DARK?

I demonstrated that products which have actually been expressly designed for global markets are very rare (especially in the food and drink sectors) and that many of the products which today can be fairly called 'global' were originally just intended for and confined to their home markets. The fact that the 'shot-in-the-dark' approach has been the start of so many of the successful global products in the marketplace today and the fact that the shot-in-the-dark approach requires the least amount of imagination, time or development effort, suggest that it will remain a popular strategy. If it is made a guiding principle that products already appearing in *one* market are evaluated in *other* markets for their ability to answer newly emerging trends and needs, we are, in fact, using a shot-in-the-dark approach to build a global strategy.

Hamburgers, hot dogs, fish fingers, chocolate-coated bars, Scotch whisky, vodka and white rum, yoghurt in pots, soft cheeses, pizzas, high-fibre breakfast cereals, and cola carbonated drinks have become global products in this way. They have turned out to be 'shots-in-the-not-so-dark'.

QUESTIONS

1. Against the first two or three markets in your response to question 4 at the end of the previous chapter, try and formulate what you would need to know about each before you could start to consider which of the alternative strategies in this chapter appears to be best for your company.

2. Analyse which kind of strategy is followed in their foreign markets by each of your main domestic competitors and in your home market by each of your main foreign competitors.

3. Given the nature of your business, consider whether its country of domicile carries a favourable or an unfavourable image in any foreign market you are operating or proposing to operate. How do you know?

7

Marketing and Management

Someone high up in the managerial hierarchy, in my view, does not necessarily get it right more often than someone lower down in the hierarchy. Blunders are made at any level.

Erik Thorn Leeson (in a letter to the author)

He who thumps his chest will soon start to cough.

from a Heineken advertisement

MANAGING MARKETING IS SPECIAL

This is supposed to be a book about marketing, not a book about management. Yet this chapter is devoted to managing. There are facets of the job of managing which are of quite specific importance when what is managed is marketing. Marketing, as I am doing my best to point out, first and foremost is an attitude of mind: an attitude of mind which I consider it to the advantage of any business enterprise to be shared by *all* the people working in that business, no matter what specific activity is made their daily task. Some in the organization fulfil a multifarious clutch of tasks which are all bunched under the label of marketing. Because the tasks which comprise marketing are so varied and because marketing is much more than just those tasks anyway, it seems useful to consider whether there are any elements in the management of marketing which need to be exposed.

AUTHORITY

'I know best because I'm the boss' no longer works, primarily because it is not necessarily and not universally true, and never has been, and secondarily because most people, especially the good ones, do not accept this kind of utterance any longer. The suggestion that the boss knows best is arrogant because it implies that, without consulting any of them, the boss's choice is more intelligent, better informed and more beneficial to the business than what any of dozens, hundreds or thousands of other people in that business might have come up with.

Good managers do the opposite. They stimulate their people to consider the choices before them. A good manager will then get some or all of them around the table to learn what views have been taken, and he may decide to give his own vision. Next he will ensure that all the viewpoints are evaluated by those concerned. Alternatives and combined views may then be considered and contingency plans discussed. Finally, the boss takes the decision, and it doesn't matter whose idea it was (though the boss will remember), nor whether the boss chooses to strive for a consensus decision, a majority decision, or, in the end, his own choice. He will state the decision; he is authorized to take it and he has responsibility for it. If the decision turns out to be wrong, he gets the blame for it. If he gets more decisions wrong than right, he loses his job.

A meeting with senior executives of Heublein was attended by the executive chairman, the senior vice-president (in charge of the main operating division) and the most junior vice-president (a young man responsible for the smallest division). At one stage I asked this junior member of the party: 'What happens if Stewart (the chairman) comes up with an idea which you or one of the others in the meeting don't like?' 'We tell him he's full of crap and then we talk about it' was the reply. The Heublein senior management of the day may not have scored high marks for diplomacy, but there was something right about the way the management worked – and it showed. People's increasingly critical attitude towards authority does not mean that we are inevitably heading for a state of anarchy. People do not refuse to accept authority, but authority has to work harder to justify itself. It has to develop skills in preventing dissent from maturing into subversion. People's increasingly critical attitude towards authority also means that they are much more interested in the whys and wherefores of authority. There is now much broader understanding for the circumstance that responsibility and authority go together than there was a decade ago. Authority has become a lot more transparent and that, in turn, means that authority can now be pushed further down the organization pyramid than previously. There is a further observation

'I know best because I'm the boss' no longer works.

about the level of management down to which authority can be pushed. Decentralization and a downward spread of authority in an organization become feasible when:

- There are a generally known policy and strategy, open communications and an informal style of management.

- There are generally known plans for operations, resulting from intensive communication up and down the organization to bring them about.

Moreover, to be crude about it, since senior managers cost more than junior managers, the more of the decision-taking you can shove downwards in the organization the more cost-effective your management resource becomes.

TODAY'S BUSINESS AND TOMORROW'S

The notion that objectives, policy and strategy should be and should remain within the confines of the boardroom dies hard. The notion is nonsensical. Worse, the notion flies in the face of the very reason for which these objectives, policy and strategy are formulated: to ensure that the business, i.e. *all* the people in it, act in unison towards known goals.

Music is composed for the purpose of being performed. Not familiarizing every person in the organization with its objectives, policy and strategy is like giving a performance with an orchestra where no one but the conductor has the score.

THE MANAGEMENT STRUCTURE

Marketing has the unique distinction of being managerially complex. It comprises a number of functional areas (thirteen, see Chapter 4). Marketing is likely to cover a range of products and can easily cover several technologically different product categories. Marketing may service a number of quite distinct distribution channels and/or end markets. Finally, marketing may have yet a further dimension to its activities: it may sell in different countries.

To illustrate, Table 7.1 shows the marketing profile for the Van Houten Company when I worked there. The breakdowns in this table are heavily summarized. Even so, the five dimensions allow for 1,260 different configurations, a fact which serves, as intended, to illustrate that marketing is a complex managerial entity.

TABLE 7.1 **Marketing dimensions at Van Houten**

Functional areas	Product planning and development
	Selling
	Distribution
	Advertising
	Sales Promotion
	Sales servicing and customer training
	Marketing research
Products	Several hundred
Product categories	Packaged grocery
	Chocolate confectionery
	Biscuits
	Fruit juices
	Industrial products
Distribution channels and end markets	Retail
	Vending
	Catering
	Industrial
Countries	Germany
	France
	Holland
	Belgium
	United Kingdom
	United States
	Singapore and Malaysia
	Japan
	Others

Various ways of coping with the managerial can of worms which inevitably occurs in marketing have been tried, but none have been satisfactory. The reason simply arises from the obvious fact that choices have to be made as to which takes priority. Look at Table 7.1 and ask yourself:

(a) Does product management take precedence over country management?

(b)   Does market management overrule functional management?

(c)   Does distribution management dominate country management?

There are no obvious answers.

There are, I am inclined to think, no subtle answers either. The solution as to how to structure the management of marketing is a matter that can only be decided by each company. The only generalizations we can make are that all the dimensions (as I have outlined them in my example) must be considered; and that, almost by definition, a 'matrix' solution will emerge (which does not absolve the company from the need to allocate priorities).

There are two criteria which, I would most urgently suggest, must be most vigorously ignored: one is, what happens to be the fashion of the day, and the other is what worked in the past.

PRINT FORMS AND RULE!

There is a common trend in companies to solve, or better still to forestall, conflict through job descriptions, organization charts and policy manuals. I am wary of these devices. They seek to legislate what a man shall do, for whom he shall do it, who he shall be authorized to ask to help him do it, and with whom he is allowed to talk (or exchange memos) and about what. By implication (sometimes expressly!) these devices also say what a man is *not* supposed to do, with whom he is *not* supposed to talk and whose help he is *not* supposed to seek. These devices, unless they are couched in the broadest possible terms, hamper communications, act as disincentives, stifle people's imagination, slow the organization down, deflect effort and energy away from the company's objectives and tend to push responsibility and authority up instead of down the organization.

If a policy manual contained policy, that would be fine. Policy should be widely known, disseminated and discussed in the organization. But 'policy manual' is a misnomer. A policy manual is a monument to bureaucracy which tells people how many days' holiday they are entitled to, who has access to the photocopier and which form to use for expense claims.

FEW LONERS

Loners in a business can be useful, but loners in marketing are rare. For things to get done and, more especially, for ways of doing things to be devised, people frequently need to get together. Nowhere is this more crucial than in marketing, because marketing covers many different disciplines and has the distinct responsibility for initiating change and innovation.

MEETINGS, BLOODY MEETINGS*

Meetings (which cover any get-together of two or more people) are a fact of marketing life. There is a mood among business people that there are too many meetings and that they are a waste of time. The mood is justified to the extent that they are a waste of time, but not in believing there are too many. If anything, there aren't enough. The inference is that there are not enough effective meetings. Let me illustrate from the negative. What are the worst meetings? The worst meetings are those held by local government. From a close and agonizing study prompted by my urge to oppose local authorities (on specific issues, not as yet in general), I have noted the factors which make for bad meetings and their inevitable consequence: wrong decisions. Consider the following:

1. The participants are chosen not for their expected contributions to the subject matter but to represent people who have little interest in and no knowledge of the subject matter of the meetings.

2. Representation is achieved not through any display of wisdom, nor even knowledge, but through visibility and perseverance among the candidates. There is no safer route to nomination than to have been the elected representative during the previous term.

3. The participants are not required to contribute knowledge or reason but an opinion, without being asked how or why it was formed.

4. The authority's paid staff will have prepared:

(a)   the decision the authority is to take,

* Title of a training film from Video Arts.

(b)   the brief for the chairman to ensure that it does.

5. Decisions, wherever possible, are postponed (see Money, under 'Motivation', p. 100). When that, finally, is no longer possible, the decisions are taken by vote.

6. Meetings are held because it is the second Wednesday of the month (except in August), not because certain decisions are best taken now.

Now if you can do no more than avoid the six pitfalls listed, you have the beginnings of effective meetings.

Meetings come in two variants: one-way and both-ways. One-way meetings should be avoided. Both-ways meetings ideally should have no fewer than two and no more than twelve people. If more than twelve is unavoidable (sales meetings, meetings of shareholders, budget meetings, for example), special measures need to be taken to ensure that the event doesn't drift off subject or off time, and that feedback is possible.

All meetings should be attended by people whose contribution is expected to be valuable and by those able to put the decisions of the meeting into effect to the extent they are not the same people. Meetings do not have to be chaired by the most senior person present. In fact in management meetings it is a good idea to have the successive meetings led by the various participants in turn. Meetings will benefit from participation by people from different functional areas and different levels of management. I need to stress this: the effectiveness of meetings will be enhanced if people chosen horizontally, vertically and diagonally across the organization are encouraged to communicate.

Meetings do not have to have a strict agenda, but the subject matter(s) must be made known ahead of time, as must be people's preparation for their contributions. Before the close of a meeting its chairman must enumerate the decisions taken and the tasks allocated, the people they are allocated to and dates for completion. These matters must be recorded and distributed to all affected.

Certain rules of the game should be imposed upon meetings to ensure their effectiveness:

1.   Make a clear statement of the purpose of the meeting.

2.   Allow only facts and judgements, not unsubstantiated opinions.

3. Do not allow anybody who hasn't done his homework to contribute.

4. Ban such statements as 'I know from experience . . .', 'because of my position . . .' or 'when we did that two years ago . . .'.

5. Do not allow people to say simply that they dislike an idea, unless they explain *why* they dislike it, and are able to provide an alternative.

6. Use every ruse to encourage creativity.

7. Use some form of evaluation of the usefulness of the meeting, to which everyone contributes.

Meetings are the most important form of communication in a company. The purposes of the communication process must never be lost sight of. They are:

- To discover as yet unexplored or to probe unexploited avenues for the business.

- To find responses to opportunities, threats or problems (and never to let the dominating power of problems encroach on the need to find and utilize opportunities).

- To create and assess new ideas.

- To use the contribution of individuals to enforce and direct the 'personality' of the business as a whole.

- To develop the communicative and managerial abilities of participants.

CHANGE AND SPEED

In 'All Change' (Chapter 11) some of the processes of change are discussed, and it is suggested that the rate of change in the business environment is accelerating.

The speed with which we are able in a company to bring change about without significantly sacrificing reliability is becoming more and more crucial. Speed in responding to change or bringing change about has become an indispensable and quite vital competitive tool. Fewer and fewer companies can escape the need to act more quickly. Thinking about ways to make a company faster on its feet in the marketplace (especially with new products) will, it is hoped, be triggered by some of the following ideas.

1. The tasks should be performed not by successive departments but by a small *team* of people. Whether the team is ad hoc or permanent, whether it handles a single task or several, and whether the people on it do so full-time or part-time depends on the size of the company and the complexity of the tasks. What does matter is that the team should carry out the whole of any task it takes on.

Such a team will be multi-functional, each member having been chosen for his knowledge of his functional area and be authorized to take decisions. The man heading the team does not necessarily have to be its most senior member, but if he is not the head of the company, he must have enough trust from his seniors to be allowed to give only infrequent progress reports, and enough weight to protect his team from the queries, interference and assaults likely to be launched at it from all directions.

The product-planning team we had at Van Houten got through an incredible programme of development work. We had to prove ourselves because we were surrounded by non-believers, especially above us on the board. We had a tiny budget, very little time and only one full-timer on the team. He was the product-planning manager and was in charge of product formulation and engineering. He also kept track of our progress. The other members were heads of sales, advertising, marketing research and design. I was their boss (during the day) and also headed the team (which met usually during the evenings and at weekends). It worked.

2. Do the *thinking first*. The time and the money goes into design, engineering and tooling. But the effectiveness of design, engineering and tooling depends wholly and exclusively on the conceptualization of what you're setting out to do. Thinking fast is good and useful but it should never be seen as a substitute for thoroughness, comprehensiveness and applied intelligence. The thinking part of the process must yield no less than a complete, accurate and detailed specification of what it is you want to present to the marketplace. (All right, in the thinking part of the process I include research, prototype making,

testing, sketches, schedules and plans.) If you don't achieve this, the designers are going to be asked to go back to the drawing board four times and the engineering boffins are going to be fooling around with a workshop full of hardware. You are going to be spending lots of money and time. Take the view that, once the specifications dictated by the marketplace are concise, immutable and complete, the design and engineering bits are easy. I know this is not the case, but take the view anyway.

3. Keep it *simple* and the steps *small*. Don't build any technological complexities or technologically advanced devices into a product unless to do so is an inescapable necessity dictated by the marketplace. If a well established device or technology will do half as well as the brilliant breakthrough the boffins have cooked up, use the former. You save a lot of time, you reduce risk . . . and there is always tomorrow (neither you nor I had expected that phrase in this book!). This blasphemous statement must be read in conjunction with the next: it makes better business sense to bring about five minor product improvements over a given period of time than one major innovation at the end of the same period. There are two reasons: you have five opportunities to interest customers against one (to bowl them over, if you're lucky). Secondly, it is far less risky, as you can adjust the thrust of your improvements as you gain feedback from each in a run of five. One big one which needs a long lead time may misfire.

4. Do *everything at once*. Our minds are geared to sequences in the way we do things. But the changes we want to bring about in the marketplace are invariably composite, if not complex. When we break down the many sub-tasks that are required, we discover that the start of one is not necessarily (and not usually!) dependent on the completion of another.

If the thinking is done first (Step 2) and there is a clear idea of where the team wants to go, a cold-blooded analysis of the component tasks is likely to show that quite a few of them can run parallel, and thus save a lot of time. Supposing we had done our thinking on the self-generating automatic banana straightener, we could simultaneously be working on consumer research, design, engineering (adjustments to machinery and production flows), getting proposals from metal die makers, advertising, warehousing and distribution logistics, talking to key customers, discussing joint promotion programmes with banana suppliers, briefing personnel, sorting out labelling and product stand-ard requirements, getting quotations from raw material suppliers, ascertaining the routes to obtaining consumer organization sanctions, selecting and training customer servicing staff, preparing a public-relations programme, and preparing costing estimates based on a range of assumptions. Given that we are in a hurry, we need to try and find out which sub-task is likely to take us the longest, so that we may lavish our resources on it first and get it on the road.

5. Use *tools*. There are outside R & D agencies, consultancies and new-product banks which can save us the embarrassment of re-inventing the wheel, and which, more importantly, can save us the time to do so. That sentence conveniently brings me to the Not Invented Here symptom. About two centuries ago I spent a day with a company that made and sold matches. Despite the fact that it sold only matches, the company was enlightened enough to recognize that it was in the 'lights' business, not in the 'matches' business. It had a prototype (which worked, I tried it) of a crystal-based device for producing sparks in lighters and had been offered first refusal on the patent for a mere pittance. The company did not take up the offer because lighters were the enemy and the idea was not invented here!

Another 'tool' which can save a lot of time is computer-aided design and testing facilities which are increasingly becoming available from outside agencies.

6. Build in *late options*. New developments for the marketplace are risky. You may not get them quite right first time. But pressure of time doesn't allow you to start all over again. So the answer is to build options into the development process (or, for that matter, into a manufacturing process) and to build them into the latest possible stages of that process so that switches can be made at the last moment to respond to the fickleness of the marketplace.

7. Finally, use *time*. We are in a big hurry. Our competitors musn't get in there ahead of us. A week has 168 hours. For something so urgent and so important why should we let 128 of them go to waste?

MOVE 'EM

In Europe generally and in Britain especially we appear to be in dread of ever dislodging people from the functional area in which, by intent or accident, they start their careers. Once a salesman, always in sales;

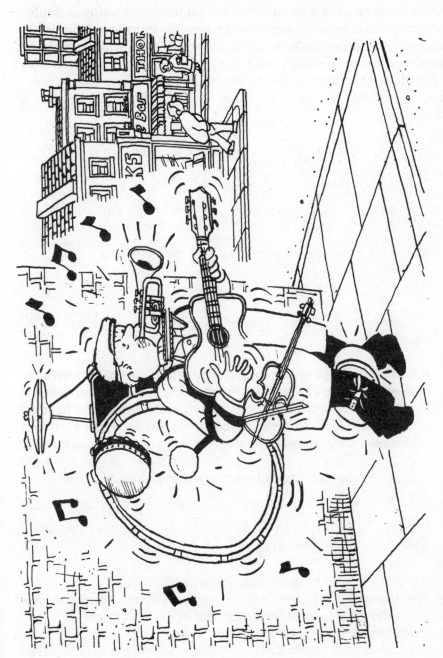

Do everything at once.

once a bookkeeper, always in accounts; and so on. Our competitors in
the Far East and even in America have different customs and quite
cheerfully move people from buying to manufacturing or from financial control to advertising. In a culture such as ours, where this cross-
functional mobility hardly exists, the advantages are not readily
apparent, but no functional area would benefit more or more quickly
than marketing. It might therefore be useful to enumerate those
advantages:

- Cross-functional mobility helps people to serve common goals,
  because they have far greater understanding of each other's
  problems; it thereby breeds solidarity.

- It broadens people's skills and interests.

- It enables a man to discover what he is really best at.

- It provides challenge to an individual.

- It contributes to people's creative skills (broader and more varied
  exposure).

- It builds a team of people who can be sent on problem-solving
  missions (as when two junior people with knowledge of five
  functional areas between them are capable of helping to fight a
  fire in a troubled subsidiary instead of having to send a very
  senior man with three helpers).

- It stretches the insights and communicative abilities of those in
  the 'host' functional area.

- It breaks down any sense of insularity, superiority or exclusivity
  which may have crept in in a functional area.

- It grooms people for general management (the more
  decentralized a company and the more organized into business
  units, the greater the demand for managers with inter-
  functional skills).

To reap these benefits requires a distinct effort. There is not normally
any urge on the part of people in a given functional area to start

moving around, so general management will have to start the ball rolling. Once the process is in train and the benefits start to emerge, then cross-functional mobility will become part of the company culture. Here are some ways to set the trend in motion:

(a) Move people around when they are still in very junior positions.

(b) Put people in multi-disciplinary project teams or working parties, and have lots of both.

(c) Give people extra-functional assignments.

(d) Run trainee programmes for young people.

(e) Encourage people to penetrate other functional areas in solving their own problems (sales manager probing a production shortfall, manufacturing man checking out product costing).

MOTIVATION

Most people are potentially able to deliver large amounts of energy and perseverance. Groups of people individually and collectively possess a great deal of knowledge, imagination, inventiveness and intelligence. All these properties are of immense value in business.

So-called experts have calculated how much of their potential people deliver to the businesses they work for in their role as employees. The figures indicate a relatively minor fraction (which I will not quote because I don't see how you could responsibly measure this dimension so as to yield accurate figures!). I do believe there is considerable potential in people which is not tapped by the companies they work for and which, quite often, is not tapped at all. That is a great pity. It is a pity in two ways: it is unfortunate for the company which has all these splendid qualities on tap but doesn't use them; and it is also a pity for the employee, because a man working to his full capacity gets more satisfaction (and fun) out of his work than a man going off at half cock.

Almost certainly the most valuable attribute a manager can aspire to is the ability to 'get the best out of his people', as the age-old phrase goes. If a manager can tap a sizeable chunk of the store of energy and qualities every one of his employees possesses, then he can be a lousy performer in all other managerial areas, but still be a good manager.

It is done by motivating people. Since motivating people is more than giving them a bigger car or 2 days at Christmas, let us briefly look at some of the ingredients of motivation.

The strongest motivating factor is involvement. If a man is fully aware of the purpose, aims and plans of the enterprise in which he works, if he is kept fully aware of his personal role in the achievement of those objectives, if he is kept up-to-date on how actual performance compares with expected performance, and if he can contribute to and is consulted about the company's future and his role in it, then he is committed to the well-being of his company. Involvement of people should be actively fostered. Nowhere is this more important and more effective then when stimulating creative contributions from people towards the exploitation of opportunities or the solution of problems.

Challenge is the next motivating factor to which many (and most of the best) people respond. Challenge, when you come to think of it, is a great indicator of confidence in a person. When you challenge a man to do something, you are saying to him: 'This is more demanding than what you have done hitherto. I believe you have the capability of tackling it'. Unless they are morons, people will respond with an extraordinary effort to succeed.

The third way to motivate people is to run training and development programmes for them. First, it stretches people's minds, and a stretched mind works better than an under-utilized one. But training and development also tell a man that there are better things in store for him, such as improved job performance, a more senior job or a transfer to a more interesting functional area.

A fourth way of motivating people is the just reward. Performance beyond reasonable expectation must be rewarded and must be seen to be rewarded. Under-performance must not be tolerated and it must be seen not to be so. Business may be fun, but it is not a holiday.

This is the point at which it is appropriate to say that a well paid man who is well motivated is much more cost-effective for the company than a poorly paid man who is not motivated. With that observation we come to money.

Money motivates. Some people are very strongly motivated by money. But as a motivator money cannot replace the first four factors mentioned. When you give money, you are likely to get your money's worth. For example, when you give 'attendance money', people attend. They have many and long meetings, they postpone decisions and they clamour for ever more elegant meeting rooms. When you give commission you get sales, not profits. You may also get price cuts, back-handers, poaching, neglect of new business development and undermining of future business prospects. When you pay for expenses, you get expenses.

Any means of motivating people must benefit the employer concerned *and* further the long-term goals of his business. If there is not this close parallel of interests, trouble will ensue. Nowhere is this more clearly the case than with money. It is argued that a man should be rewarded in relation only to the factors which, in the execution of his job, he can influence. I do not disagree. Which is why I cannot understand why so many salesmen (and not a few sales *managers*) are still rewarded through a commission on sales (whilst they should and can affect profit!). The close parallel I mentioned, it seems to me, is nicely achieved when good performance is rewarded through the award of shares in the company.

THE CULTURE

I use 'culture' to describe the way people behave towards each other, the mores, traditions and standards they apply, culminating in 'the way we do things here'. The culture in many companies is the result of happenstance – nobody has ever given any thought to the company's culture or style of doing things. Culture *does* matter because it facilitates communication between employees and it helps shape the 'personality' of the company, which is so important in the competitive world outside. Anyone attending a conference or seminar will have listened to delegates from another company in discussion among themselves and will not have failed to notice how their style is quite different from one's own company's. About both Philips and Unilever, people have said to me: 'You don't just work there; you join a religion'. Since culture matters it is worth being conscious of it and it is worth realizing that it can be deliberately influenced or changed. Notice what happens if a new, forceful chief executive joins a company from outside.

If the corporate culture is important and if it can be influenced and changed, it is worth discussing whether, and, if so, how, it might be changed. Some dimensions that might crop up in such a discussion are the following. Hot air – do we tolerate it or stamp it out? Should we be more or less formal? Do we ignore, tolerate or encourage creativity in people? How do we deal with the Poor Old Freds who always try and usually fail? How do we value (and show that we do) intelligence or

The way we do things here.

knowledge? How do we deal with subversion? Are we better than or challenged by our competitors? How about our ethics?

MANAGING ASSETS

Without people, a business is an untidy heap of hardware. People are the most valuable and the most crucial asset a business enterprise can aspire to. That is why the management of people must not be left to chance, custom, routine or formula.

The next three chapters deal with the second most important asset of a business: knowledge. It too needs management; often it doesn't get it.

QUESTIONS

1. When you try, objectively, to analyse how much authority (your own and that of those around you in the company) is derived from an ability to communicate with and stimulate subordinates and how much from 'position', hoarded knowledge, power or company politics, how does your organization stack up?

2. Can you think of new ways of disseminating policy and strategy among all the people in your business?

3. Can you think of (new) ways of bringing as many as possible of the people in your business into the process of making policy and strategy without risk of creating a free-for-all chaos?

4. Your company will have found some way of tackling the functional/product/market/country matrix configuration. How well does it work? What are the obvious snags? How would you set about devising improvements?

5. One way of reducing reliance on organization charts, job descriptions and policy manuals is to check how often they are used to solve problems. Another is to do without them. Have you tried either?

6. When you consider the points made under 'Change and speed' and 'Move 'em' in this chapter, what elements could you use in the running of your own business?

8

Knowledge, Its Architecture and Management

What men daily do, not knowing what they do!

William Shakespeare: *Much Ado About Nothing*

KNOWLEDGE FOR MANAGERS

This chapter talks about management *knowledge*, i.e. knowledge, as distinct from data, facts, information or intelligence. It explains that it is knowledge, rather than merely those other factors, which business managers need properly to do their job. It also goes into the criteria which must be used in putting knowledge together – for those I use the word architecture. Finally, it argues that the process of constructing knowledge in a business needs not only to be managed but managed with a marketing attitude of mind. A marketing approach to the supply of knowledge requires the definition of the market, the identification of needs which exist or are anticipated in that market, and then the conception and design of benefits aimed at satisfying those needs.

Now a business enterprise is in fact faced with a variety of 'markets' for knowledge. There are a whole series of quite distinct groups of people who deserve, or indeed require, to have knowledge about the company: shareholders, moneylenders, employees, government, suppliers, the trade and the company's neighbours are examples of groups of people who each have their quite specific requirements for the knowledge they expect from the company. It is in the company's own interest, as well as in the interests of these various publics, that that knowledge is provided truthfully, comprehensively, intelligibly and quickly. How that should be tackled is not the subject of this book. This book, in this and the following two chapters, is concerned with yet a further group of people – the company's managers – and the knowledge they need. Managers have their own distinct, far-reaching (and

[105]

forward-reaching) requirements for knowledge. Managers cannot be fobbed off with knowledge designed for such other groups of people as shareholders or fiscal authorities.

KNOWLEDGE – THE VITAL INGREDIENT

As an ingredient in the process of managing a business, knowledge has gained in importance both in absolute and in relative terms. Its importance to safeguarding the survival of the business now supersedes that of skills in such areas as manufacturing or marketing.

The success of a business becomes identified more and more with knowledgeability, be it in (product or production) technology, marketing, staffing, finance or procurement. Whereas data, information and know-how can be and are bought in from outside, knowledge is generated within the business. Awareness is growing that the generation of knowledge cannot be contracted out. Other things not long ago considered inherent in the conduct of the business are now beginning to become the subject of make-or-buy options. We are witnessing the emergence of businesses which are sub-contracting manufacturing or selling and distributing in order to concentrate their resources on the development of a clearly defined area of knowledge.

Conversely, we see companies, indeed whole industries, going into decline simply because they have failed to collect the knowledge which would have enabled them to shape their own futures.

CAUSES OF FAILURE

An examination of the most prevalent causes of failure in companies shows how lack of appropriate, adequate and timely knowledge has in all cases been at the root of those failures. Consider the following points:

1. In an earlier chapter a company's dependence on groups of people was discussed. When a company no longer meets the wants, needs or expectations of one or more of these groups, as is the case when it is ignorant of those wants, needs or expectations, its survival is threatened, and continuing ignorance will bring the company down.

2. A company's product offering is under continuous attack from its competitors, and insufficient awareness of competitive activity can spell disaster. That competitive threat is at its greatest when it comes from outside the company's own industry. Customers do not buy production technologies, they buy benefits, and so if an outsider comes along with the offer of greater benefits or the same benefits on more advantageous terms by using a wholly new or otherwise unrelated technology, customers will turn to the outsider. Ignorance of technological developments in traditionally unrelated industries is therefore a cause for company failure.

3. Companies fail because they wake up too late to the fact that their performance is at variance with what was expected. Not identifying quickly that the company is deviating from its planned performance or not meeting budgeted targets are causes for failure.

4. Companies fail because their costing is not able to show them the fixed cost contribution provided by incremental sales; their pricing either fails to provide that contribution or rules out those incremental sales.

5. A company may fail because it enters a new market or a new area of business activity without a thorough insight into precisely what competitive scenario is established there and how it can form a distinct competitive advantage in that market. If a substantial investment has been committed to the new activity, that lack of insight will mean the demise of the company.

6. A cause of failure which frequently occurs in small, rapidly growing companies (and often very profitable ones at that) is that management has failed to make forecasts of amounts of money (or money's worth) flowing out and into the business, or that it has failed to make such cash-flow forecasts with a sufficiently short interval of time.

It is not suggested that it is in all cases easy to provide the knowledge which will forestall these six typical causes of company failure, but it is imperative to do so nonetheless. (The typical reasons for failure given above have come partly from our own observations and partly from work down by McKinsey and Company.)

CHARACTERISTICS OF SUCCESSFUL COMPANIES

Having identified lack of knowledge as the cause of typical failures of companies, it is valid to examine the attributes of successful companies. McKinsey and Co. have identified the following six characteristics. Again in each case it is the generation of relevant, adequate and timely knowledge that has been behind the success factors. Successful companies perform in the following ways:

1. Identify and emphasize more effectively than their competitors the key success factors inherent in the economics of their business.

2. Segment their markets so as to gain decisive competitive advantages.

3. Base their strategies on the measurement and analysis of competitive advantages.

4. Anticipate their competitors' responses.

5. Exploit more or different degrees of freedom than their competitors.

6. Give investment priority to types of business that promise a competitive advantage.

KNOWLEDGE AS AN ASSET

Because of its great and growing value, I consider knowledge the second most important asset (after people) a business can strive to build. The term 'asset' is used very deliberately. An asset is something used as a *resource* in business and something which has *value*. Knowledge meets both criteria – comfortably. But the term 'asset' in the parlance of business has acquired connotations which need to be challenged.

For nearly two centuries bookkeepers have deceived us about 'assets', and we have let them get away with it. To have assets is A GOOD THING, bookkeepers have told us, and I wouldn't disagree. But 'assets', bookkeepers have gone on to say, must be things you can see and touch, and assets must have a value capable of being expressed in amounts of money.

One must take issue with both these requirements. Adherence to them can in fact give rise to labelling as 'assets' things which many a good manager would probably wish to do without. Taking an admittedly jaundiced view, here are some of the things bookkeepers call 'assets':

- Stocks, when a lot of money has been tied up in a faulty sales forecast.

- Plant, when it comprises an irrevocable investment in a market prediction made by someone long since dead or retired.

- Buildings, when they comprise an investment unrelated to their market value, in the wrong place and used for the wrong purpose (such as a sit-in or a lock-out).

- Debtors, when, as always, they consist of a group of people who are having a free-of-charge ball on our money and who we are afraid to restrain.

Accuse me of nit-picking about what we do, or do not call assets. Ask 'What's in a name?' Argue that it doesn't matter.

But it *does* matter, for two reasons:

1. The first thing managers are told about their tasks is their responsibility for the well-being of assets. Managers, accordingly, care for assets – clean them, polish them, keep them cool, hot, humid or dry, grease them, add to them or take them out to lunch, as the case may be. On the other hand, items that don't appear as assets in the balance sheet don't get that kind of care and attention. They remain unorganized, undeveloped and unmanaged – very often unnoticed. This is why companies look after their computers, typewriters, filing cabinets and adding machines, but not after their knowledge, know-how, skills and creative ability, or their development and the training of staff in them.

2. The second reason why the designation 'assets' for things does matter is that managers are quite happy to invest in them but not in things which are not designated as assets. Managers happily invest in machinery without questioning whether by any chance there is already over-capacity in the industry; they will extend credit to customers for a mainstream product without wondering whether a bit of

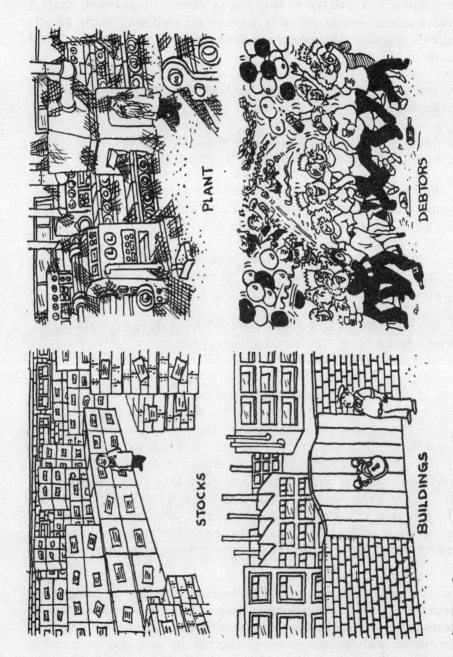

Assets . . . ?

extra development might take that product out of the mainstream; and, lured by the hum of a running mill, managers will lock up working capital in stocks well beyond any reasonable sales expectation without a search for complementary products to put through the marketing organization.

The consequence of managers' behaviour vis-à-vis things called assets as opposed to their indifference to things not thus labelled is that investment tends to be lavished on tangibles which other people – competitors, for instance – can also buy. Investment in 'assets' (in the bookkeeper's context) does not, by and large, provide the company with uniqueness.

What gives a company a competitive advantage are things which *do* make it unique, innovative, technologically advanced, quick on its feet – in short, inimitable. These attributes are not generally the immediate result of investment in what bookkeepers call assets. They spring from human attributes such as intelligence, creativity, courage, per-severance, energy, imagination, audacity; from the provision of the breeding ground for these attributes within the organization; and from the development and vigorous use of knowledge.

CHANGES IN THE BUSINESS ENVIRONMENT

It has been suggested that knowledge for business management has been gaining in importance and that it is continuing to do so. The growing importance of knowledge has not come from the explosive growth of data sources or the tremendous development in data-processing technology. Those are just tools. Rather, the growing need for knowledge has come about because of the following quite sweeping, rapid and continuing changes in the business environment:

1. An increasing number of companies are experiencing competition from new competitors. We in the 'developed' countries have put some money, skills and management into the 'developing' countries in order that they might bring forth goods and services to serve their own and world markets. The world is quite a small place in terms of those who are able to pay for the goods and services which are on offer. So if steel, textiles, ships, shoes, air transport, confectionery, radios, yachts and cameras are suddenly offered by the developing

countries, the producers of such goods in our countries feel the pinch. Those companies in the 'developed' countries which are aware of what is happening need knowledge:

(a) to incorporate technological improvements in their product which the new competitors cannot match, and

(b) to diversify into new business activities.

2. Many reputable companies have come under sharp attack at their annual meetings from vociferous minorities of shareholders. Housewives boycott food stores. We have strikes, walk-outs, secondary picketing. Environmentalists and nuclear-energy opposers block factory gates. There is an increasing array of hitherto silent groups of people who are suddenly making demands, requiring a hearing, or affecting the operation of our businesses.

Since it is generally more productive to have discussions with such groups of people before they start throwing bricks through our windows, rather than after, it becomes necessary to know what goes on in the minds of employees, customers, public-action groups, consumerists, shareholders, unions, the trade, and local, regional, national and international government.

3. In several West European countries governments now manage a larger part of the national economy than all of private enterprise put together. Governments manage through legislation rather than through managerial ability, and so business is being subjected to an ever-broadening stream of new laws. Knowledge is required, both to comply with legislation which has been passed, and to help forestall, redirect, amend, postpone or improve legislation which is in the pipeline.

4. All the world's natural resources are running out. Most are running out gradually. What does not occur gradually is the fear of a particular resource running out in the absence of an obvious alternative. That fear crops up suddenly and causes a slowing down or drying up of supplies or an increase in price. The oil crisis, the cod war and the herring ban are examples. Political manoeuvring can be another cause of diminishing supplies, as can climatological disasters. It is not suggested that it will always be possible to mobilize the knowledge to foresee these curtailments but, in some instances, improved alertness could have saved some companies great embarrassment.

5. We are witnessing a change in the way good managers manage,

It is generally more productive to have discussions before they start throwing bricks through your windows.

in response to increased emancipation of workers, growing employee independence, and demands for greater job security and job satisfaction. Here too both deeper and broader knowledge of what is in the minds of employees, would-be employees and employee representatives has become mandatory.

6. Most companies serve markets in which customers are better informed, less gullible, more self-determined, more critical and fussier than before. Customers now accept, or indeed require, innovations with ever-increasing rapidity. To keep abreast of these changing needs is a condition for survival in business, and to bring them about a condition for success. Mass consumption is dead. The mass production of the personalized product offering has become the industrial challenge. Market segmentation has become the imperative strategy for every business and it can only be based on intimate knowledge of what moves every customer.

7. The final change is self-generating. As the importance of knowledge becomes more widely recognized and the tools with which to generate and distribute it more readily available, so its use as a competitive weapon is becoming more forcefully used.

This, then, is a scenario of recent developments in the demand for management knowledge.

KNOWLEDGE VERSUS EXPERIENCE

If you accept that 'experience' is the accumulation and digestion of information, trial and error picked up on man's walk through life, then the main difference between it and knowledge is that the latter is selective, capable of extending into the future and imparted in an organized way under pressure (of time). Experience is a splendid school, but the courses are too long and the fees are too high. The rate of change in the environment is so great, the number and variety of sources so vast and the 'ingredients' required so varied that experience alone can no longer equip today's manager. Experience is too slow and its reliance on trial and error too expensive. No manager, irrespective of the stage of his career, can avoid putting time and effort into the absorption and generation of knowledge. The alternative is losing his managerial qualification.

THE GAP BETWEEN INFORMATION TECHNOLOGY AND MANAGERS' NEED FOR KNOWLEDGE

This chapter is about knowledge, not about the tremendous technological advancement in the tools with which to locate, harvest, sort, store, process and present information. But the tools are tangible and knowledge is not, so the two tend to get confused. Human nature is like that. Society's response to new technologies is not always very wise or even rational. Inventions like gunpowder, the motor car, steam, nuclear energy and now electronic data-processing have not, in all cases, provoked the most responsible responses.

A more harmless but illustrative example of the way people tend to respond to technological innovations is given by a Tribal Chief in Darkest Africa. He ordered an immediate replacement of his black-and-white TV set when news of the invention of colour TV reached him. There is no electricity in Darkest Africa on which to run either and the nearest transmitter is 1,300 miles away. But to stay with the times, the Tribal Chief had to have colour.

The breathtaking developments in information technology have obscured rather than exposed the need to manage knowledge. The emphasis seems to be on the wondrous tricks each of the new tools can perform rather than on the management decisions and plans which it ought to be the only purpose of effectively integrated knowledge to support.

Business management is becoming aware of the need for knowledge. What is not commonly appreciated is that knowledge, like any other resource, needs to be acquired and paid for in terms of time, effort, and money. Of those three, as usual in business management, money is the most readily allocated, and, without further ado, is spent on data-processing equipment and the experts to work it.

What tends to happen is that by allocating money to hardware and operators, senior management thinks that it is absolved from any responsibility to organize knowledge, and the data-processing experts are left to process data – and that they do. The change that has taken place is that management still isn't getting the knowledge it needs, but it now costs a lot more money.

Two grave errors of judgement have been committed:

1. Management has complacently assumed that knowledge would be served up in handy packages without any need to get actively and critically concerned with its architecture, without analysing its own

Tribal chief had to have colour.

actions and plans in terms of the specific knowledge required for their support in each case, and without realizing that the inertia of knowledge requires a continuous intellectual effort on the part of the user as well as the supplier.

2. Management has failed to make it crystal clear to all concerned that *it* is the customer, that its decisions are the only recognized 'market' for knowledge, and that all those concerned with the collection, storage, assembly, retrieval and presentation of any or all of the elements of knowledge are supposed to be performing a market-orientated service.

Investment in information processing *per se*, rather than enhancing the quantity, the quality or the speed of management knowledge, in fact tends to widen the gap between those in a company who manage and don't understand the technology and the technologists who don't understand management. The interests and motivation of the two groups of people are radically different, and the chances that they will drift further apart are far greater than that they will converge.

It is knowledge rather than the tools to process it which is the *real* asset.

KNOWLEDGE IS INERT

The transfer of knowledge is a laborious process. Even if there is willingness both on the part of the supplier and of the recipient, the communication of knowledge is like swimming in treacle. It is sobering to realize that the sun's energy and the resources on or near the earth's surface could easily provide adequate nourishment for the world's population, if only the knowledge to utilize those resources could be more effectively diffused. Knowledge is inert, and vast amounts of energy are needed to spread it around; so, meanwhile, millions of people starve to death.

QUESTIONS

1. What are the main 'markets' for knowledge your company has to cater for? What are the main criteria that knowledge must meet in

each case? How would you define the purpose which
management knowledge must serve?

2. Assuming some of the shortcomings of the information system in
your company are not unfamiliar, are you able to identify any of
the four managerial shortcomings as particularly relevant? If so,
can you devise ways of grappling with them?

9

An Anatomy of Knowledge

Grace is given of God, but knowledge is bought in the market.

Arthur Hugh Clough: 'The Bothie of Tober-na-Vuolich'

AN EXERCISE IN HOUSEBUILDING

I am using the word knowledge quite deliberately to distinguish it from 'data' and from 'information'. Knowledge is the ready-to-use support base for management decisions to act or to plan action. Its characteristics are that it is *relevant* (to the action), that it is *complete* (i.e. it contains all the elements needed for the decision and is free from unnecessary elements), and that it is *comprehensible* to the user (i.e. the one taking the decision). 'Information' may be relevant and complete (in fact, it may contain a surfeit of elements), but it has not been made comprehensible to the user (it is not ready-to-use for that reason). 'Data' are simply untreated elements to which no selection, screening or processing has been applied. The difference between 'knowledge' and 'information' is the architect. 'Information' is the total of all building materials delivered on site, 'knowledge' is the house awaiting occupation, and 'data', to complete the analogy, is what you find at a builders' merchant.

The analogy is deliberate, not merely to illustrate how unsatisfactory it would be to expose the family to living amid piles of building materials, but to highlight the relation between the occupier and the architect. The latter builds to fulfil the needs of the former. No matter what constraints may be imposed by the limited resources of the occupier, the architect has to deliver some sort of dwelling ready for occupation.

The architect's role is a very conscious one. His actions are wholly goal-directed.

[119]

It is my contention that management knowledge in business needs to be built from data, trends, analyses, estimates, evaluations and judgements from every relevant source in much the same way as a house is built from bricks, mortar, timber, pipes, wires, tiles and glass into a functional whole. Such a functional whole can only come about if there is design and management. In the building of a house the architect produces the design and supervises the efforts of various contractors and the quality, specifications and quantity of the materials used.

NO ARCHITECT

Most businesses struggle along with what they euphemistically term 'information systems', which have come about accidentally in the course of their histories and are no more than a poorly co-ordinated set of monitoring disciplines. There is no design for the system as a whole nor any element of management; the architecture is lacking.

PRODUCT-ORIENTATED

Such parts of corporate information systems as are managed at all are managed by people who are production-orientated. They are the accountants, researchers, lawyers and EDP specialists. They produce accounts, research findings, legal documents and computer print-outs. The other parts of the system, which are not managed at all, tend to produce rumours, press clippings, ill defined problems and other irrelevancies.

The information system in many companies is a heritage of non-interlocking routines, interspersed with odd items, haphazardly collected in much the same way as the merchandise at a bring-and-buy sale. (You bring what you don't want, you buy what you don't need.)

The systems are built on the technical criteria which are relevant and interesting only to the producers of information, without heed to the needs and capabilities of the users of information: the people who manage the business. In my office every week we get a dozen brochures offering courses, seminars, books and conferences on such subjects as 'Understanding data processing', 'How to read research findings', 'Accounting for the non-financial executive', and such-like.

We never hear of seminars for EDP people, researchers, lawyers or accountants on such subjects as 'The information needs of managers', 'How management works', or 'The ingredients for decisions'.

HISTORY

Information systems are built to show, often very accurately, how the business has been performing in the (immediate) past. Moreover, an important part of the system, the accounts, is built to account to people who have no part in managing the business at all. Accounts account to shareholders for dividends, to the Inland Revenue for tax liability and to Customs and Excise for Value Added Tax. Accounts may tell management about some past mistakes, but nothing about what will be right for the future. Yet the future is the only period over which management has influence. Similarly, marketing-research data are mainly geared to monitoring what happened in the past. Very little is (as yet) specifically designed to uncover probabilities for the future.

TRADITIONAL BUSINESS

Information systems are built to show the performance of a (long) existing sphere of business activity, without questioning the future success of that type of business, without heed to the axiomatic truth that one day that type of business is going to run out of steam. Many of our companies, and most of our governments and labour unions, display alarming symptoms of tunnel vision by continuing to invest their own and other people's money in business activities which are no longer capable of generating adequate returns. Companies which are very exacting in the organization of information with which to run their existing business, when they *do* realize that new business activities need to be developed, frequently base their decision to enter that new business environment on the most superficial information. In my experience there is no major area of business management endeavour in which greater blunders are made than in diversification moves. Invariably lack of thorough knowledge about that new sphere of business is the cause.

ONLY QUANTIFIED

Information systems are built to show business performance in quantifiable dimensions – mainly in financial terms. Information systems
tend to be exclusively geared to express business performance in terms
of yields on capital invested. A systematic appraisal of the company's
performance in terms of its non-financial aims and responsibilities is
generally omitted.

UNPACKAGED

Information systems tend to supply data to the user, the operational
manager or the business strategist, in a raw or semi-finished state. The
user is assumed to be a do-it-yourself fan. He has to refine, to select and
to determine priorities and risk factors before he can formulate the
choices before him.

Nearly every business decision or plan needs to rely on information
from several sources and disciplines. In most companies, however,
information suppliers are mono-disciplinary. None of them are trained
to think in multi-disciplinary packages of information, or even to
consider other disciplines or their sources. The accountant, the engi-
neer, the researcher, the EDP manager and all the others, moreover,
each use their own jargon, their own standards, tolerances and definitions. It is up to the user of information, the business manager, to:

(a)   Think of all the sources of information that are relevant to his
      problem, and then work out which disciplines to tap to obtain it.

(b)   Put up with widely divergent definitions, standards and degrees
      of accuracy from the respective disciplines.

(c)   Translate and reduce the jargon-laden information he is given to
      something he can comprehend.

(d)   Analyse, sort, correlate, weigh and discount the data he was
      given and put it all together.

These are not activities the average business manager is frightfully
good at. Neither is he paid to do them.

Since this is such a common and serious shortcoming, let us look at a
few illustrations:

- The information to back up plant investment proposals tends to lack marketing information in depth.

- Strategic plans tend to put heavy emphasis on marketing, financial and technological information, but they are short on information about manpower requirements.

- Information about likely (regional, national or international) government action tends to be short-supplied in many diversification programmes.

A POOR LUBRICATING JOB

Information systems suffer from stagnation symptoms. Like lubricating oil in an engine, information has to circulate fast and furiously if it is to do its job. If oil should fail to circulate in an engine, that engine is reduced to scrap in a matter of seconds. If a similar lot should befall a business, it is likely to outlive that engine, but not for long. Two circumstances hinder the unhampered flow of information in business:

(a) The fact that information or knowledge, under certain conditions, can mean power. This can lead people to keep knowledge to themselves till they feel they can derive maximum power from imparting it.

(b) The difference in motivation between the supplier and the user of information. The supplier of information tends to look upon himself as a professional (accountant, researcher, lawyer, psychologist, economist, or whatever) and indeed he is encouraged to do so. He has difficulty in concealing his disdain for the manager's preoccupation with the effectiveness of everyday operations. Conversely, the business manager has not the slightest interest in the skills and procedures that go into the presentation of information, so long as he gets the relevant knowledge quickly and in a usable format.

MUDDLED GENERATIONS

Information systems do not adequately allow for the circumstance that information needs arise at different levels of business activity and planning. Information is needed to bring about immediate improvements in plant efficiency or traffic control. But information is needed also to plan the company's activities in 6 years' time. There are different generations of decision-taking and there should be different generations of information to support each. The generation of decision-taking dictates the time-span; the breadth, the depth, the degree of heterogeneity; the accuracy, the interval and the delivery period of the knowledge required to support it. An accurate analysis of the pay-out of last month's promotion for 'ZIZ' washing powder, on its own, is of precious little value in determining the point in time when the company should be geared for a relaunch of the 'ZIZ' family of powders. Failure to relate the structure of knowledge supplied to the generation of decision-taking it is required for results in waste of effort and lack of co-ordination between demand and supply.

FAILINGS SUMMARIZED

To summarize, the shortcomings of existing information systems in business can be put down to only four failings by business management:

1. It has failed to proclaim that it – management – is the only legitimate customer for management knowledge.

2. It has been bad at asking the right questions and at steering information suppliers towards the right catchment areas.

3. It has failed to insist that the supply of knowledge is an integratory function, since few management decisions can rely on single-source data.

4. In contrast to the way it treats production and marketing (to mention only two), management has failed to put its information function under management concomitant with its importance as a business asset.

These failings point to a lack of both the architecture and the management of knowledge in business.

QUESTIONS

1. How often do suppliers of information (or, with luck, knowledge) in your company discuss with management the adequacy and appropriateness of what they supply? Can you think of any ways in which you could help along what this book calls the architecture of the knowledge in your business?

2. If you are a manager, please think carefully and list all the kinds/ sources/types of knowledge/information/data which you used in each of the last three important choices you made (OK: decisions you took).

3. Assuming you are aware of your company's real competitive strengths, can you transpose that strength back to the knowledge which underpins it? Are there any, however tiny, gaps in that knowledge?

4. Again looking at your last three important management choices, how would you evaluate the knowledge you had available in terms of:

    (a) Accuracy of the least accurate constituent?

    (b) Cost (against effectiveness)?

    (c) Timeliness?

    (d) Competitiveness?

10

The Tasks for Knowledge

Whether failure is due to hardware, software or tupperware, ultimate responsibility must always rest with people, both because we built the stuff in the first place and because we are the only ones with a stake in how things turn out.

Arthur Bloch: *More Murphy's Law*

ARCHITECTURE

The architecture of knowledge is necessary because we are dealing with the building of a complex, multi-disciplinary service system. Moreover, once built, architecture will need to adapt and alter the system in response to the way the business it serves grows and changes.

Management of the system is necessary to ensure its quality, adequacy, efficiency and cost-effectiveness. The system requires management for precisely the same reasons that a factory, an office or a sales force require management.

THE MAIN CRITERIA FOR THE ARCHITECTURE AND THE MANAGEMENT OF THE INFORMATION SYSTEM

1. The system needs to be designed from the user backwards, not from the producer forwards. The user is the customer: his needs are central to the whole being of the system and crucial to its success.

2. The design of the system should run from the trunk of the tree to the boughs, from the boughs to the branches, and from the branches to the twigs – not the other way round. The design must start with the

needs of the company's top strategy-makers and management and move from there to the lower levels of management. Only in this way can the two following common failings in corporate information flows be discouraged:

(a)   There is no organic channel through which information for strategy-making can flow downwards or upwards along the various levels of management.

(b)   Higher management gets fed only the information which lower management wishes to impart or which lower management believes it wishes to hear.

3. The system needs to be designed to provoke ample thought and consultation about the company's strategy and plans. It does so by providing insight into probable environmental developments.

4. Since no information system can provide all knowledge about everything, the system should not be designed to provide the fullest information where the company meets its greatest problems, but where it is most successful and where its greatest future opportunities lie.

5. The system should be designed to scan as well as to probe and analyse.

6. The system should be managed to recognize the inherent problems of communication between managers and the information people. If there is a demand for knowledge of any complexity, there should be intermittent contacts between the information suppliers and the customer (the manager) to ensure that the supplier (a) remains on course and (b) does not supply a more extensive or refined package than is needed. In sourcing and harvesting the constituent information, the information supplier should start with sources which supply broad, shallow information quickly and cheaply and gradually work towards narrow, deep, time-consuming and expensive information as and if needed (see Figure 10.1).

FIGURE 10.1   Information sourcing and harvesting procedure

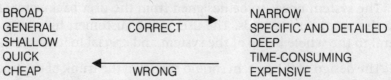

A lot of detailed, time-consuming, expensive marketing research that is bought could readily have been replaced by desk-research findings if only someone had thought of it.

7. The system should be designed and managed to provoke speedy, if not instant, management action.

8. The system should be designed to signal unplanned and unforeseen events and their sources, and to support management in responding to them quickly.

9. The architecture and management of the system should anticipate clashes of interest and power games between managers and offer procedures to solve them. This type of problem arises especially in matrix-type management patterns in the larger companies.

Architecture of knowledge – summary

Design from user backwards.
From trunk to twigs.
Promote thought about strategy.
Focus on strengths and opportunities.
Scan, probe and analyse.
Communicate knowledge to suit 'customer'.
Start with broad, general, shallow, quick, cheap.
Provoke instant action.
Pick up unexpected signals.
Anticipate human misbehaviour.

A MARKETING JOB

The information function in business will answer user needs only if those responsible for its architecture and management are possessed of a *marketing* attitude of mind. The marketing man is not the fellow who merely supplies what the market *wants*. Instead he is the fellow who probes, searches and tests to discover what the market *needs*, and who then sets about to provide the things that will answer those needs, making a profit while doing so. There is a colossal difference between wants and needs. In our case identifying wants for information is a simple matter of going round the people who use it and asking them. To discover the *needs* for knowledge that exist in a business is a much more demanding exercise. It requires a very thorough understanding of what the company's aims are, how it operates, what its strengths and weaknesses are, and what relations it strives for with all the groups of people in its environment. Furthermore, it requires an insight into the way decision processes work and into the way people communicate with one another.

Marketing people have devised 'convenience' foods in various forms. What they have done, in effect, is to replace toil, time, dirty hands, washing up, gas, electricity, and risk of failure, by additional processing in the factory. Instead of processing as far as the kitchen, they are processing as far as your plate.

Information should be marketed like convenience foods. For example, instead of unloading various unco-ordinated batches of unprocessed data at the backdoor of the sales department, a composite package of integrated, processed information should be presented to Joe Bloggs, the sales manager, at the precise moment when he has to take a specific decision. It will mean that Joe will have more time for the job for which he is presumably best suited: that of managing his firm's selling activities. It also means that the important job of collecting, analysing, correlating, and presenting information is done by people who are trained to do just that.

DIMENSIONS AND DIRECTION

The design of a company's management knowledge system has to take account of two sets of dimensions: the internal/external ratio and the past/future ratio.

1. The internal/external ratio

Sources of information from which the company must derive its knowledge lie outside the company and within it. Clearly it must draw on both. However, the company which has seen no great changes in its product mix, its technologies and its markets for, say, 5 or 10 years will need, deliberately and forcefully, to strengthen the sourcing of its external knowledge. It will probably experience little urge to do so. The company which is in the midst of diversifying, making acquisitions or otherwise bringing about a great deal of development in its activities, or which has recently been doing so, will need, deliberately and forcefully, to strengthen its internally sourced knowledge. It too will not experience a very strong need to do so. In both these, extreme, cases the design of the management knowledge system must provide what does *not* come naturally, because it is the availability of knowledge which must *precede* (and provoke) management action to change its focus. It is knowledge which must persuade management in the introspective company to be more outward looking, just as it is knowledge which must persuade the expansive company to focus on consolidation.

2. The past/future ratio

Knowledge of past performance is the principal means that companies have of measuring:

(a)   How close they have come to what everyone had reason to expect.

(b)   How good or bad management has been at planning and why.

Measurements of plant utilization, gross wages, market share, cost of raw materials, and debt servicing costs fall into this category.

Assuming that companies are not aiming in the immediate future to go into liquidation, the other knowledge component is knowledge about the future. Here is a paradox. The more predictable the future is, the easier it is to plan for it and acquire the knowledge to make those plans. The more predictable the future, the less effort is required for planning and the less importance needs to be attached to it. Conversely, the less predictable the future, the more difficult to acquire the knowledge with which to plan the company's survival, yet the more vital it is to devote time, effort and intelligence to planning.

In today's 'age of discontinuity'* insight into the future has become so vital that management's preoccupation with it has started to outweigh the importance of past-performance monitoring. Planning is an activity that can no longer be left to planners but has become the everyday concern of managers at all levels. It is clear that the emphasis on the need for planning indicates a need for knowledge about the future. The knowledge, by definition, is largely non-factual: it will consist for the most part of guesses, estimates, probabilities, judge-

* Title of a book by Peter Drucker.

ments and assessments; and mainly 'soft' data of the kind for which data-processing technologists do not show great affinity.

3. Focus on strength

Good management will have defined the company's main strength (its area of excellence) and will be the trend-setter for the company's style. Both strength and style are dynamic and require constant development, adaptation, testing and even experimentation. Management must be confident, in addressing itself to these matters that its relevant knowledge is at all times second to none.

PROFIT CENTRE?

This book argues in favour of building a knowledge-providing asset rather than an information function. To do so, that building process requires architecture and the asset managment. Finally, knowledge suppliers must have a marketing-orientated approach to their task. Since marketing is the identification, anticipation and satisfaction of user needs profitably, where does this profitability come in?

The answer in principle is simple enough: to make the supply of knowledge in a company a profit centre. The ground rules are the same as when purchasing, manufacturing, product management and selling are made profit centres. Business, after all, has already become acquainted with buying/selling time, R & D effort, computer time and software, legal counsel and consultants' time. No responsible business would fail to cost its knowledge-related activities, purchases and indirect costs. Why lump them all together into an indifferentiated overhead charge? Why not charge out the cost of knowledge to the user? Even a crude attempt at doing this is better than the flat-rate overhead charge. The very real advantage is likely to be a first-ever awareness of the cost of knowledge in relation to its use. The integral cost of information in most companies today is a very elusive item. Awareness of the (approximate) cost of knowledge must stimulate efficiency in the way it is used. All functional areas and every single department in a business are both suppliers of data and users of knowledge, and therefore an inflow and an outflow of man-hours, machine time, data purchases and overheads can be costed and priced, even if only approximately. In addition, time and effort will be expended and purchases made to procure data and information from outside the business, which, again, if it is not actually invoiced, can be costed. Finally, time, equipment, skill and managerial input will be devoted, within departments and in a central information unit, to processing the data and information obtained into the knowledge required. Here too the monetary cost can be approximated and the worth to the user negotiated with him.

I am quite convinced that only through operating the knowledge-generating asset as a profit centre will it be possible ever to get close to achieving the optimal mix between the conflicting factors of action-orientation, accuracy, reliability, timeliness, comprehensiveness and cost. The accountability for the money's worth of information procured and knowledge supplied which the profit-centre approach imposes will ensure that four tenets of information effectiveness are achieved. These tenets are the following:

1. The accuracy and reliability of a package of information is only as good as that of the least accurate or reliable component.

2. The cost of information, or the cost of additional accuracy of information, should never exceed the risk incurred when action is taken without it.

3. Approximate data or estimates delivered on time are always better than accurate information which arrives too late.

4. A complete package of approximate information is always better than an incomplete package of accurate information.

The process of bringing a company's knowledge system up to date is a matter of attitude as much as methodology and technology. In the absence of willingness and determination to apply a contemporary rather than an Edwardian outlook on knowledge management, no amount of gadgetry or techniques will increase its effectiveness; it will merely increase its cost.

THE ARCHITECT'S TASK

If a company does want to develop its knowledge into the asset it ought to be, it will need intellectual effort and energy to do so. Whether that task is undertaken by an individual full-time or by a group on a project basis does not matter a great deal. The essential attributes for the team or the individual are precisely those of the architect: a profound understanding of the purpose to which the building is to be put and an intimate knowledge of the materials used and the construction methods applied.

The architect of management knowledge does not start out on completely barren terrain. There is a past. There will be items of knowledge which have been especially useful or conspicuously lacking, as the case may be. There will be a history of successes on the one hand and blunders on the other, and people's recollection of how knowledge played a part (or failed to play a part) in each of these events will provide pointers for the composition of knowledge in the future. If the company has gone to the trouble of analysing what it is good at and what it is bad at, it will almost inevitably have decided whether to add strength where it is strong and whether to circumvent its weaknesses, overcome them, compensate for them or ignore them. These choices, again, will yield quite unambiguous guidelines about knowledge which needs to be to hand. Elsewhere in this book it is argued that well managed companies determine their objectives, mission, policy, strategy and plans. These things, more than anything else, provide a framework for the architecture of the knowledge in the company.

However, the architecture of knowledge needs to go further. Knowledge in a business enterprise is not an end in itself. Its purposes are to help people to do things, provoke them to do things, alert them to the need to do things and enable them to plan to do things. Knowledge is a tool.

An obvious way to shape management knowledge would seem to be to go and ask the people who are supposed to do something with it what they want. Obvious as that might seem, it is not the way to set about it. Managers cannot be expected to be so versed in information sources, in information-harvesting techniques, and in sifting, weighting, processing and presenting information that they can provide any reliable or useful guidance to the knowledge architect.

WASHING POWDER

A marketer wishing to launch a washing powder would be wasting his and his respondents' time if he discussed the formulation of the product with the housewives he is hoping to sell his product to. Instead, he or his marketing research agency will be interviewing a representative sample of housewives about their washing habits, the benefits they are looking for in the powder they use and the merits and demerits of the product they are currently using. The basis for finding out about washing-powder characteristics from users (housewives) is getting clean, soft, fresh smelling clothes back in the cupboard with the least amount of fuss. It is in exactly the same way that the correct formulation of knowledge for managers is arrived at. The basis of it is the competence and confidence which managers have when they do what they are supposed to be doing: weighing alternatives and taking decisions for action or planning subsequent action.

TAKING DECISIONS TO BITS

Making a manager talk about his decisions and plans in terms of the knowledge used in each case is a daunting task. He has never in his life looked at information, data and knowledge as if they were neatly arrayed before him. When asked about supporting knowledge, he will mention two or three identifiable sources, and after that his memory will appear to have dried up. Likely as not at that stage he will come up with '. . . and of course I knew from experience'. When the manager mentions his experience, he intends it as a knock-down argument. But, as was argued earlier, experience is nothing but an untidy heap of observations – a multifarious collection of facts, circumstances and responses – which people have encountered while promenading through life. There is no great merit in the acquisition of experience – all it requires is an ability to survive, and time – whereas the acquisition of knowledge is a worthy achievement. Experience does not stretch the mind in new directions. Knowledge – its extent or its direction – is in no way limited by who wants to acquire it.

It is easy and tempting to applaud and stimulate the development of knowledge and dismiss experience as an inferior attribute. But first we must consider the bumble bee.

As every zoologist knows, the wing surface of the bumble bee, given its body weight and its inability to beat its wings more than 200 times a second, does not enable it to fly. The bumble bee, however, does not have this knowledge; it has only its experience and that allows it to fly quite happily.

The inescapable and uncomfortable conclusion is that we cannot dismiss experience. They only thing we can stop, or rather the thing we must try to stop, is its use as a knock-down argument.

In dissecting managers' decision-taking processes the task of the architect of knowledge is not only to uncover and identify the supporting sources of information the manager remembers but also to harness, probe, question and analyse what its owner calls his experience. Without the fullest insight into the adequacy of the tools the manager has currently to hand, it is not possible to design better tools.

To extract all this information from managers is tedious and frustrating, and makes the questioners unloved. The good news is that the more often one goes through the process, the more one understands the manager's mind. Eventually one gets results. The current organization of knowledge in most businesses leaves plenty of scope for the benefits of conscious knowledge architecture to become readily evident.

QUESTIONS

An organization which has succeeded in building the kind of knowledge-generating asset which this chapter describes will, at frequent intervals, answer 'yes' to the following questions; a checklist:

1. Does the system provide the company with such quality and scope of knowledge about its chosen area of excellence that it can retain leadership in it?

2. Are catchment areas for information, both within and outside the company, identified and adequately covered:

    (a) As far as the company's future objectives and plans are concerned?

    (b) As far as the company's plans and its stance vis-à-vis its stakeholders are concerned?

    (c) As far as monitoring current performance is concerned?

3. Are requests for knowledge in the company always expressed in terms of the plans, options or decisions which that knowledge is required to support?

4. Has an analysis of the company's strengths and weaknesses been extended to point to any areas where new knowledge needs to be gained?

5. Are steps being taken to identify all the supply and demand responsibilities for knowledge and to organize and manage their interaction?

6. Is a 'marketing-orientated' attitude being fostered among those whose primary task is the supply of knowledge?

11

All Change

Not 'What will tomorrow look like?', but 'What do we have to tackle today to make tomorrow?'

Peter Drucker: Preface to *The Age of Discontinuity*

ONLY CHANGE IS CONSTANT

The overriding need for knowledge, which we have just looked at, has arisen from the accelerating rate at which changes take place in the environment in which all businesses operate. The people who are today the senior citizens of business management are the first generation of managers who have consciously faced the challenge of having to manage change. The rate of change in the business environment has been and still is accelerating. In the 1930s people marvelled at how, in 40 years, motorized land and air transport had been commercialized from nothing to world-wide predominance. Today world-wide predominance of technical products is realized inside 5 years.

It is often argued that people resist change. I believe this is too hasty a judgement. If people have reason to anticipate benefits from change, they will show no resistance to it at all. Obviously if people expect an impending change to be to their disadvantage, they will resist it. What people also resist, and what fills them with anxiety, is uncertainty about the outcome of an impending change. This last observation determines people's attitudes to change in general. Those attitudes differ radically and can be categorized as follows:

(a) Change is ignored. Head firmly in the sand, life-styles are continued – wherever possible unmodified.

(b) Change is attacked or obstructed. Because of their anxiety about

[139]

the possible outcome of change, any change is resisted by people with this attitude.

(c)   Change is responded to by adaptation to its effects. Reluctantly or otherwise people will take cognizance of change and consciously determine how they will live with it.

(d)   Change is deliberately brought about. Rather than waiting for change to come upon them, people actually bring about or contribute to change.

The anatomy of change will be further dealt with in Chapter 14, The Hierarchy of Choices. Here it is sufficient to say that the four attitudes to change outlined above are ranked in order of decreasing uncertainty about the outcome. They are thereby also ranked in order of decreasing risk, exemplified by the ranking of these attitudes showing an *increasing* measure of influence upon the exact nature of the change and its effects.

A private individual, depending upon the specific event we are dealing with, may well survive quite happily by ignoring or fighting certain changes in his environment. He may well get away with no attempt at adapting to change (there seem to be quite a few individuals in that category!) and he is absolved from any pressing need to bring change about. But a business enterprise has no such easy options, because it is expected to survive and therefore must be wary of taking avoidable risks, and because it has a multitude of quite specific responsibilities to groups of people in its environment (see Chapter 3, People). A business enterprise cannot afford to ignore any changes in its environment. It must perform a deliberate scanning job and operate early-warning systems to identify and evaluate changes as soon as they appear (Chapter 15, Planning Is Not Dead). The enterprise may in isolated cases decide to resist or fight change, but only if it has failed to come up with or rejected all alternative courses of action and only if it can reasonably expect to achieve results.

An enterprise will very frequently need to adapt to change, and it has a duty to exploit change as often and as forcefully as it can. The opportunities for exploiting change increase the earlier change is spotted. But the greatest predictability of the outcome of change, the lowest risk and the greatest chance of benefit from change arises for its originator and architect. To bring changes about must remain the purpose of a well managed business.

TRENDS FOR MARKETERS

More by way of examples than through any attempt to be exhaustive, here are some trends that are already affecting the actions and plans of thousands of marketers:

1. There are irreversible changes in the mode of people's work; there is a shift from work requiring brawn to work requiring brain. This has far-reaching consequences for people's requirements for nourishment, clothing and exercise.

2. Through shorter working hours, longer holidays and high unemployment there are changes in people's requirements during their non-working time.

3. Rapid increase in people's real spending power.

4. Steady increase in education standards and in the educated proportion of the population, coupled with an explosive growth in available information and the tools to harvest it.

5. Greatly increased passive and active mobility and cross-cultural exposure (passive: it comes to you in your armchair; active: you go out there to seek it).

6. Strongly increasing sense of independence, self-assertiveness and vociferousness. Business is becoming aware of its accountability to groups of people it never heard from in the past.

7. Changing attitudes to authority, to society, to the environment and to health.

8. Consistent and rapid change in the balance in a very fast growing world population, with the proportion of 'developing' peoples (mainly coloured) increasing and getting poorer and the proportion of 'developed' people (mainly white) decreasing and getting richer.

9. Household sizes in the developed countries shrinking fast.

10. Role of government in society becoming increasingly dominant.

11. Growing polarization within the distributive trade: multiple organizations of large, general stores with their ever increasing buying power on the one hand and the emergence of an increasing variety of life-style orientated, mainly smaller specialists on the other.

RENEWAL

There is hardly a page in this book which doesn't either discuss or advocate change in the managing of a business. The need for change is argued in several other chapters, as are the reasons why that need arose.

Management is responsible for bringing change about in the operation of its business in response to changes in the threats and opportunities in the business environment. Change which is brought about deliberately by managers must aim at improvement. As such, that change can legitimately be described as renewal . . . or innovation.

INNOVATION – A BUZZ WORD?

The word innovation, like just about every word in the marketing vocabulary, is much newer than the business practice of renewing what one does and how one does it. Innovation, the practice, goes back to the dawn of human endeavour. Man has always sought to better himself, his environment, his dependents and his competitive position against others. Indeed nothing stimulates man more to innovate than competition, irrespective of whether it is competition for material circumstances, social status, artistic performance, craftmanship or business achievement.

Innovation in business as we know it today is a very down to earth, necessary business function, aimed at securing the survival of an enterprise. Innovation in business is not an add-on or an extravagance. It has become the everyday concern of every business manager. Innovation is not synonymous with diversification. Innovation in the 'core' business, as it has come to be called, is just as crucial as innovation through movement into new business areas. Often it makes good sense to carry on innovations in both spheres simultaneously.

WHENCE THE IDEAS?

Ideas are legion. There are patent offices, inventors' agents, exhibitions and idea banks full of brand new, original product ideas. It is extremely unlikely that, during the next quarter of a century, any new product gaining market prominence will not be based on an idea, a concept, a design or a prototype that is already in existence today. Product ideas take a long time to come to commercial fruition:

The aerosol can was invented and tried in 1926, the self-service shop in 1931, and the ballpoint pen in 1888. Clarence Birdseye discovered food freezing in 1924 and that discovery was only because the Eskimos had been doing it for untold years already. The safety pin dates from 1849 and the dishwasher from 1889.

Appealing and indeed romantic as the idea of creating wholly new ideas may be, the practice of inventing, developing, industrializing and commercializing a new product – in that sequence and all by the same people – is extremely rare. The breakthrough idea tends to come by accident to people who are not looking for it, or on purpose to people who do not have the ability or the means to exploit it commercially.

We tend to use the term innovation only for products. But it is just as relevant to use it in relation to other marketing-mix elements: distribution, selling, advertising, packaging or sales servicing. We can justifiably speak of innovation if nothing truly new happens at all, but if the innovator is the first to apply a new marketing mix using existing ingredients. The explosive growth in the sale of computers started when someone advertised machines in the Sunday glossies and sold them by mail order. The widespread food service from pubs resulted from pubs' loss of drinks business as people, more and more, drank at home. The huge 'package holiday' business sprang from the underutilization of existing transport and accommodation facilities.

There is no correlation between the commercial success of an innovation and the creative or technological brilliance on which it is based. When you think about it, that is obvious. Commercial success derives from an ability to respond to customer needs, but brilliance derives from the talents, cleverness, ambition or imagination of an inventor. Unless the latter is assiduously applied to the former, the two will remain unrelated. Chapter 6 gives an analysis of 'new' products in the UK retail food market, 85 per cent of which were either imports of existing products or anglicized versions of existing products in other countries. The inference is obvious: if you want 'new' food products in the UK, go and look abroad.

I can find nothing dishonourable in applying an existing technological or product concept in a new, hitherto untried way – even if it is not as glamorous as inventing the wheel – as long as it does not result from downright theft. Computers were developed for scientific purposes. Does that detract from the usefulness of the cheap thing you carry about like a briefcase? Bar coding was developed for grocery retailing, but would that make it any less useful as a tool for librarians? Doorstep delivery was developed by milk retailers. Why should it not be stretched to include other household needs?

It is sobering, but it should be an inspiration for every marketer, to think that many of the great innovations in the world of commerce have come from applying a technology or a product concept used in one industry/market environment to an entirely unrelated industry/market or to both concurrently: the use of lighting oil in the new combustion engine, the use of electronic chips in timepieces, the use of petrol stations to sell umbrellas, and the use of waste cooling water (as from nuclear power stations) to farm fish are examples of such cross-conventional applications.

It needs inquisitive minds, deliberately provoked scanning, suppositioning, testing and a great deal of discussion to spot opportunities of this kind.

NOTHING NEW – JUST BETTER

Whilst they hardly qualify as innovations, considerable improvements can be made in existing products or services without fundamental changes at all. There are dozens of opportunities, so many that the fifteen below took me as long to think of as it did to write them down:

1. Sardine tins in sympathy with their openers.

2. Stamps which tear along the perforations.

3. Banks that keep customers' hours, not bankers' hours.

4. Table knives the weight of whose handles keeps them on your plate, not on the floor.

5. Doorknobs far enough from the doorpost to leave the skin on your knuckles.

6. Cigar bands which can be removed without tearing the cigar apart.

7. Pockets in trousers capable of retaining their contents when the wearer is comfortably seated.

8. Locks on car doors which need more than an amateur thief and 20 seconds to crack.

9. Insurance suppliers who inform you what you're buying when you are buying and don't wait to do so until they fail to meet your claim.

10. Portion packs which may be opened without decimating their contents.

11. Plumbers, electricians, carpenters and decorators who say they'll come and do.

12. Unsegregated radio and television programme guides giving details of all programmes.

13. Shampoo bottles designed to stand up in bathrooms rather than to take up unwarranted space on grocery shelves.

14. Labels on wine, whisky, honey and cheese which tell about the taste of the stuff inside.

15. Airlines whose use of bigger planes in the air does not penalize customers by forcing them to spend ever more time in queues on the ground!

What I consider to be one of the most brilliant innovations in retailing of all time is the freezer centre (a form of food retailing thus far confined to the UK), invented by John Apthorp in the late 1960s. Its brilliance lies in the combination of five discernible, if not obvious, circumstances:

(a) Sales of frozen foods were increasing faster than food sales generally.

(b) People with freezers bought a lot more frozen foods than those without, but only 3 per cent of households had freezers.

(c) Frozen food was shrouded in mystique, and a lot of people were suspicious of its attributes.

(d) To all intents and purposes there were only three manufacturers, all very large, who produced products in (small) retail packs. Those three dominated the retail market, making the cost of entry into that market prohibitive for any other frozen-food supplier.

Labels which tell of the taste of stuff inside.

(e) In the catering sector of the frozen-food market there were dozens of mainly small manufacturers who between them offered an enormous product range in bulk (large) packs which commanded relatively low prices.

So it was that Bejam was quickly successful with its chain of shops which sold freezers and frozen foods and gave away freezing know-how, exploiting the availability of very broad product ranges at relatively low prices from manufacturers that had earlier been debarred from the retail trade.

HOW NEW IS NEW?

No, the state of technological advance of an innovation is not necessarily linked with the likelihood of its commercial success. To work towards commercial innovation, those responsible for it must be in no doubt about what state of newness they are trying to bring about. New can mean quite different things to different people. There are six distinct ways something can be 'new':

1. A new (cheaper or better) way of manufacturing or selling an existing product. Using robots in the manufacture of motor cars or mail order to sell made-to-measure clothing are examples.

2. A new (or additional) positioning for an existing product. The savoury snacks manufacturers had for years positioned their products to appeal to young people. Then one manufacturer broke out of that mould with a sophisticated range of products in better quality packs to sell to adults at premium prices.

3. Line extensions, modernization, redesign or a target segment adjustment in existing markets. All these innovations frequently occur in the motor-car market.

4. 'New-for-us'. This means a new entry in an existing market. The product is new only for the suppliers. A market exists for the product hitherto serviced by other suppliers. The belated adoption of electronics by mechanical watchmakers illustrates this situation. Mars' entry into marine electronics is another example.

5. New market/application/usage. An existing product is taken to an entirely different (for it: new) market or, within its existing market, a wholly new application is found (and promoted) for it. The compact disc was developed for computer-connected data storage. It was subsequently realized that the same technology (and indeed manufacturing facilities) could be used to produce a superior substitute for the gramophone record and audio tape (and video tape, for that matter) – a case of both a new market and a new application. An example of a new usage is the extension of jeans and gym shoes worn by young people from leisure and sports apparel to everyday wear.

6. New, new. The new product is new for everybody, for everybody that is with a role in the marketplace: the supplier, the market, the target consumers, the trade and the competition (as well as the market

researchers, the advertising and promotion consultants, the legislators and the media). Electronic toys, the Rubik cube, expanded polystyrene and weight-watcher clubs are recent examples.

It is curious to note that novel combinations of existing ingredients tend to come to market much more quickly than products based on new technologies. The latter lie about or are hawked around for years or decades before they are commercialized.

There are good reasons why it is necessary to be precise and unambiguous about what is meant by 'new' in new products. First, knowing what is new and exactly for whom it is new directs the energy and communications effort to where they are most needed. Secondly, it enables the marketer to identify his new or changed competitive environment; he knows who and what he is up against. Thirdly, the extent and complexity of newness is directly related to the riskiness of the enterprise. The more that is new and the more groups of people it is new for, the greater the gamble the innovator takes and the greater also, quite often, his rewards if it works.

Hundreds of consumer products labelled as 'new' do not come across as such because consumers are not able to perceive (or told) what is 'new' about them. 'New-for-us' products are sold as 'new' when, by definition, there is nothing *new-for-them* about them. It is legitimate to sell 'new-for-us' products as 'new' only if it is essential to let customers know 'we have finally caught up with competition'. Under all other conditions it is better to think of an alternative selling platform.

New application/market launches require the innovator to realize that his product is totally unfamiliar to his prospective target audience. When electronic pocket calculators first came to the mass market, the suppliers of these handy gadgets did nothing to enlighten consumers about their functioning. Instead they confused their prospective customers by twaddle about 'suppressed zeros', 'fully floating decimal points' and 'automatic overflow indications'. The potentially interesting market for Citizens Band radio was ruined from the start because the suppliers failed to demonstrate how those tools should be most usefully and responsibly used.

FAILURE

You hear about the high failure rate of new products. 'Nearly 73 per cent of all new grocery products in the US failed within a year' or 'Eight out of every ten new products developed during the past 5 years failed' are typical of statements about the hazard of new product development work.

But such statements are so woolly as to be meaningless. First of all, is it actually the *product* which failed? It is unfortunate but very common practice to omit a cold-blooded, critical post-mortem of why the performance of a new product has been disappointing. That disappointment is certainly not invariably the result of inadequacies of the product *per se*. Quite different errors may have been the cause.

The positioning of the product may have been wrong, its attributes being communicated to the wrong group of people. The timing may have been wrong – the product may have just missed a trend or a season or it may have been ahead of its time. The package design may have been wrong, failing adequately to tell consumers about the new product. Advertising may have been to blame, spelling out an irrelevant message, using the wrong media or having been inadequately funded. The product may have been poorly distributed or it may have been distributed through a channel where customers would not be looking for it. Even promotional tactics may have caused the failure of the unfortunate product: promotions bring about connotations and ideas in consumers' minds, and *should* encourage trial of the product, but the wrong connotations or ideas can put consumers off a product.

Failure of a new product is costly and demoralizing. Both these effects can be softened and the failure exploited if its causes are identified. To paraphrase Theodore Levitt and enrich Sod's Law, 'If you don't know where you went wrong, you'll go to that place again'.

The second question which needs to be answered is *What is meant by failure?* Is it failure to reach a certain sales target or rate of sale, failure to get a certain rate of distribution or level of re-ordering, or failure to achieve a certain share of the market? Is it too great a dent in the sales of existing products? Perhaps it's failure to recoup investment in the new product, failure to reach profit targets, or failure to win over a specific group of customers?

Failure may result from unrealistic or carelessly set targets or objectives. To strive to win a substantial share in a mature market dominated by one or two brands with a 'new' product which is not significantly different from the brand leaders would constitute an unrealistic target and invite failure. (It happens quite commonly!) To set a sales target without refinements as to positioning, target audience, advertising and promotion targets, minimum distribution levels and a distribution channel strategy is careless. Such a sales target, with all its loose ends, is almost certainly out of reach.

Clarity about precisely what yardsticks are applied with which to measure the performance of the new product actually enhances the chance of its success, since corrective action can be accurately directed.

PLANNING

In the foregoing sections it has been argued that innovation should be regarded not as a frivolous luxury but rather as a down-to-earth and essential business function. It must therefore be planned, and what needs to be planned is not just the innovation but also the dissolution or replacement of what went on before. Obsolescence must not be allowed to overtake the marketer; he has to plan for it. Product planning thus becomes not only the programming of innovations of any kind but also the programming of the phasing out, adaptation, updating or replacement of existing products.

A product is a means to an end. The end is a composite of objectives, which includes profitability, jobs and the continuity of both. Planning is about making resources perform to achieve objectives. Product planning shows how resources are used to achieve objectives by discovering and filling the needs of a market.

The curious thing about the performance of a product for its supplier is that that performance can only come about if the same product at the same time performs satisfactorily for the customer. The two types of performance are measured by entirely different yardsticks. A product may perform splendidly for its customer and, at the same time, perform poorly for its supplier. The MG sports car was an example of such a product.

The inverse, though, does not apply. A product must answer the needs of some customers from its first appearance on the market, even if at that time it is still far from meeting the supplier's objectives.

To be one of the first suppliers in emerging markets often means sacrificing product performance in the short term. At the same time, for the 'early adopters' the performance of the product in their terms is likely to be very significant and they become very ardent and deliberate customers. Servicing those 'early adopters' – and this applies to customers for aeroplanes down to those for grocery products – often constitutes an excellent long-term investment.

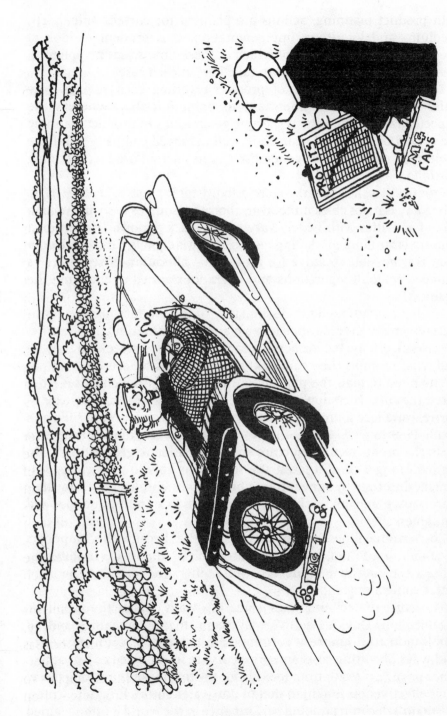

The MG performed satisfactorily for its customers – poorly for its maker.

In product planning, actions are planned for current and short-, medium- and long-term implementation. It is prudent to look at product planning in terms of which of these time-scales it applies to, since quite disparate actions are called for in each case.

The three 'generations' of product planning each require very different actions. It is important to point out that, whereas the expected results from the respective generations of product planning are spread over several years, any well managed company will have projects of each of those generations in its current product-planning portfolio.

Product planning and the responsibility for it must be central. In no other way is it possible equitably to allocate resources to so dissimilar a mix of activities with widely varying pay-back periods. That product planning must be a marketing responsibility is equally clear, since only then is it possible to strive for an optimal allocation of resources as between ongoing operations and operations aimed at changing the business.

We have mentioned the dissimilarity of the product-planning projects which are likely to appear in a planning portfolio at any one time. It is useful, briefly, to look at what each type of project seeks to achieve and what prompts the need for change in the first place.

The need to plan the phasing out of existing products arises from three reasons. The supplier, by cutting back market support expenditure, can bleed a product to death and derive a useful cash fillip as a result. Planning will enable the supplier to reallocate the resources tied up in the product's manufacture and distribution to greatest effect. In his own longer-term interest the supplier is able to protect his customers' interests by preventing a build-up of obsolete stock in their warehouses and by enabling customers to continue to service old equipment.

The terminal illness of products rarely arises because their suppliers do something to make them less acceptable. Almost invariably customers lose interest in products because other products which perform better come along.

The cause of declining sales is nearly always outside the supplier's organization. Obvious as this may seem, many companies, indeed whole industries, ignore it. Too often internal searches are instigated to find ways of cutting costs and price cuts are introduced as a panacea. Since price cuts result from looking for the trouble in the wrong place, their effectiveness is akin to that of hot-water bottles for curing colds.

Britain's declining trading performance in the world is often blamed on a low average new product performance by British industry. The criticism is probably justified. To find the causes for this low average performance is not easy.

More so than in the countries with which Britain competes, there appears to be a tendency for companies to define their business in terms of the physical properties of their products or manufacturing processes rather than in terms of the functions their products perform for their customers. Examples are companies which state their business to be carpet-making, distilling, aluminium-extruding, insurance, or cosmetics, whereas what they actually sell is home comfort, enjoyment, weight/maintenance saving, confidence and hope respectively.

In quite a number of markets in Britain there is a relatively high degree of concentration both among suppliers and (trade) customers. Under these circumstances it can be in the mutual interest of a large supplier and a large customer to maximize sales of a particular product, both parties being attracted by the sizeable contribution to fixed costs generated by the high volume of that product. It is not exceptional in these cases for suppliers to rob smaller (newer) products of (some of) their (gross) profit in order to maximize the marketing support available for the high volume product. It is no surprise, when this happens, that any new product activity suffers.

Redesigns, relaunches, new sales and distribution methods, repositioning, range extensions, and adjustments in the product/service mix are all part of updating a product. Relatively speaking, updating programmes are low risk, quick and cheap, and every product/market relation should be under continuous analysis to reveal updating potential.

Supplementing existing products has, as its main purpose, to stretch a particular resource so that additional revenue may be generated without materially extending the resource in question. If a sales force can handle additional products, if a promotional programme can accommodate an extended range of brands, or if a factory has the capacity from which an additional group of customers can be serviced, then obviously the incremental cash flow will greatly enhance profitability.

Replacing existing products is the obvious companion of scrapping them. The life-cycle has two ends; no product can live profitably for ever.

Finding new products with which to replace existing ones is a task of an entirely different magnitude from updating or supplementing existing products. The development of replacement products is risky, expensive and time-consuming. The high cost of financing this kind of development can only come from the profit generated by the product which the new development is destined to replace; there is no other source. The lead time is governed by the need for the new product to be generating profit at a rate no less than the fall-off in the profitability of the old product as it reaches maturity.

If that is accomplished, the company has merely managed to stand still. It means that the replacement product must come to market before the old product's profitability has levelled out. A useful rule of thumb is that the replacement product should be launched at about the time the product it will replace has reached its maximum *rate* of profitability. The implication is that product replacement, and the flow of funds needed to finance it, are set in motion for each one of a company's most successful products. It is a situation which operational and financial managers, typically and understandably, find very hard to swallow.

Both extensions of and complete changes in a company's main business activity are matters which will occupy the minds and dictate the actions of an enlightened management. Moves in either of these directions are much farther-reaching than the developmental processes discussed hitherto, because changes in the main activity of a business means that changes in the resources of the business must be planned. Retraining people, replacing plant, relocating the business, and changes in policies and procedures are some of the things which will need to be done.

Extensions beyond the traditional kind of business activity may be sought simply because the company considers there are additional opportunities to be grasped. Alternatively, a company may discover that its original type of business is being threatened, and so a spreading of risks rather than immediate higher yields is the motive.

The effect of political or economic action by countries which supply raw materials, the emergence of industries in developing countries (which can only live by exporting to rich nations) and the disappearance of indiscriminate mass consumption in the markets of the Western world are three factors which are posing threats to many of our industries.

QUESTIONS

1. Make an inventory of all the competitive products which sell in
    significant volumes and which have been launched as new
    products (or services) during, say, the last 3 years and then:

    (a) Determine how 'new' they were?

    (b) Find out where the concept for that new product came from
         or how it was generated?

2. If you and your customers had unlimited authority, what
    improvements in your products would you work out between you?

3. When was the last change made in the choice of distribution
    channels handling the company's products? Have any of your
    competitors gone elsewhere since? Have you experimented with
    new types of distribution channel since then?

4. Can you think of 'other' industries (than your own) that could ever
    pose a threat to your company through the use of their
    technology for a product with which to replace yours?

12

The Product Life-cycle

Life is just one damned thing after another.

Elbert Hubbard: *A Thousand and One Epigrams*

A CAVEAT

The great age which that chestnut the Product Life-cycle has attained is suggestive of the deference we owe it. Because of the continuing usefulness of this concept, a description of it belongs in this book.

A caveat is in order, however. Despite its name, parallels between the behaviour of products (or brands or companies) in markets and the lives of human beings are best avoided: there are too many fundamental differences and inconsistencies between the man-made lives of products and those of people.

Two generalizations can be made about the useful (i.e. profitable) life of products in markets:

1. The life-span of all products is continually decreasing.

2. Products from areas characterized by a high rate of technological development, fashion products and discretionary-choice-type products have relatively short lives, commodity-type products have relatively long lives. The Rubik cube was conceived and born, lived its extravagant and highly cosmopolitan life, aged and died in little more than a year. Coal, as a source of power, has been with us a few hundred years, and looks like being around for a while yet.

As I am using it in this chapter, the life-cycle concept applies to products in markets rather than brands. The concept covers the total value of sales of (and the total profit generated by) a particular product irrespective of how many suppliers participate in the market.

A TOOL

The ultimate significance of the life-cycle concept is, one hopes, that it provides the marketer with an additional tool with which to manage his business. Costly mistakes have been made in marketing through failure to recognize symptoms, and an insight into the product life-cycle concept would have gone a long way to prevent those mistakes being made.

There are not many concepts in the marketing arena which have come in for quite as much abuse as the concept of the product life-cycle. Mainly that abuse stems from the criticism that there are so many practical examples of products which have defied the life-cycle. You then discover that the reason those products have freed themselves from the life-cycle pattern is because someone has been clever enough to do something to their positioning with the very purpose of forestalling their maturity symptoms. The life-cycle concept tries to tell you what will happen if the positioning of products in markets is *not* drastically changed. There is an analogy with the trip computer in a modern car. It will tell you when you will get to your destination, provided you continue to drive the way you have been driving. If you are not satisfied with that predicted time of arrival, you can change your style of driving to improve your actual time of arrival. But having made that change you can hardly blame the trip computer for getting your original time of arrival wrong.

The product life-cycle derives its usefulness from the circumstance that it allows the marketer to determine, with reasonable accuracy, a set of typical characteristics of the market in which he operates and the ways these characteristics are likely to develop if no significant changes are brought about in the marketing activities of the suppliers which operate in that market. Conversely, an insight into the product life-cycle concept will help a supplier in a market determine what changes in his marketing mix at what point in time are likely to be the most effective. More important still, a marketer able to plot his product's position in relation to its life-cycle will be able, with reasonable accuracy, to predict when its profitability is likely to level out and when it is likely to go into decline – again on the assumption that he makes no drastic changes in the positioning of the product. Working with the product life-cycle concept provides the marketer with an early warning system which tells him at what future date changes will have to be made or replacement products will have to be available. In Chapter 11 I explained how the need may arise to make considerable investments in development and marketing of a replacement product at the very time when the product it is meant to replace is at the zenith of its profitability. The product life-cycle concept will help to sway the disbelievers and authorize the funding for those investments.

PHASES

The product life-cycle concept sub-divides the typical product's life into five phases, called here Development, Pioneering, Rapid Growth, Maturity and Decline, as shown below.

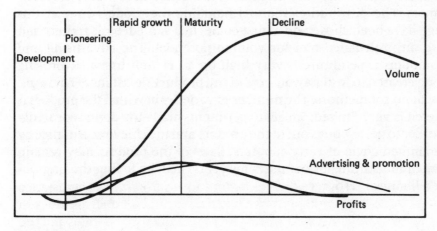

Product life cycle.

1. **Development**

The first phase describes what happens before anything appears on the market. Time, effort and money are spent on an idea or a concept, sometimes in substantial quantities. There is a possibility that this investment will not be recouped from the product that results from all this backroom work. The product may miscarry. However, for the product that is successfully launched, this backroom work will be highly significant, since it determines to a large measure the amount of time needed for competitors to enter the market on a me-too basis. Obviously the higher the investment needed to enter the market and

the more technically complex the product, the greater the lead over
the competition is likely to be. However, the greater the novelty of the
product (and this need have no relation to the investment that went
into its development), the longer it tends to take to penetrate the
market.

2. Pioneering

The introductory phase, from the moment the product first appears on
the market, is one of slow growth and low volume. Unless the originator deliberately chooses to play it alone for as long as possible, unit
price is high. Penetration is low and confined to what Prescott called
the 'early adopters',* the original, quite deliberate, innovative consumers. The distribution channel handling the product may at this
stage have been chosen on a 'first come, first served' basis rather than
with any calculated aim for volume potential. The advertising and
promotion expenditure is very high on a per unit basis, advertising
being created to foster awareness of the product's existence. There are
few or no competitors. The number of varieties in which the product is
offered is very limited; in fact experiments are being done repeatedly
in order to get the bugs out of the product and to achieve acceptance by
the limited circle of early adopters. Sales of the product may remain
limited to this category of users for years, heavily taxing the originator's financial resources.

3. Rapid growth

Then, sometimes fairly suddenly, sales begin to accelerate. Quite frequently the early adopters, who are rather deliberate users, cause the
use of the product to become something of a status symbol and the
resistance to change in habits of other consumers begins to
break down. Even before imitative competition starts, the originating
company may have to lower prices to enhance penetration of the
product into broader user categories. Rapidly increasing volume
begins to enable the originating company to realize attractive margins
of profit; in fact during this stage unit profit tends to reach its maximum as increased volume begins to enable economy of scale benefits

* Raymond Prescott: *Law of Growth in Forecasting Demand* (1922).

to be reaped. The properties of the product have become stabilized. Total advertising and promotion expenditure rise rapidly during this phase, although decreasing on a per unit basis. Emphasis will shift from creating awareness towards the achievement of a maximum sampling effect.

Depending on the amount of protection (through patents or sophisticated technology, for instance) the originating company has obtained, the rapid growth in volume and the high profitability will form a pressing invitation to imitative competition. Penetration in the original distribution channel tends to become complete towards the end of this phase; price competition by that time has started to bring down unit price and unit profit with it. Total profits may continue to grow a little way into the next phase. With the rapid increase in the number of competitors, however, maximum profitability for any of the early entrants in the competitive race is likely to have been reached and passed during this phase, throughout which the sales curve is concave. Level or declining volume growth rates mark the beginning of the next phase.

4. Maturity

During this phase the competitive jockeying for position starts in earnest. Competition, like the law of the jungle, sifts out the weaker brands. Whilst product differentiation for the basic product diminishes, proliferation of types, sizes, colours, flavours and models starts. Full penetration of the consumer market is achieved, and, for durables, replacement sales are gaining in importance. Unit prices come down sharply in the early stages of this phase, levelling out towards the end of it.

Market shares of the big brands tend to grow as the cost of market entry now increases relative to the per unit margins available. New distribution channels are opened, adding to the diffusion of product ranges carried by the various sectors of the retail trade. Per unit rates of advertising and sales promotion will drop further, as will total expenditure for the product category as a whole towards the end of this phase. Promotional themes show a strong trend to brand claims: dealer promotions gain in relative importance and so does merchandising. New entries into the market are few near the end of this phase; in fact fewer competitors remain than there were at the beginning. When sales growth rates dwindle to nothing, this denotes the final phase.

Customers are bored.

5. Decline

Customers are bored. The product is no longer exciting. In the case of durables the market is made up almost entirely of replacement sales. Consumables are fighting a losing battle against more up-to-date substitutes, or are simply failing to reach younger consumers. The number of competitors decreases. The drop-outs not infrequently mark their death rattle by severe price-cutting. Competition amongst the survivors does the rest to bring about a substantial drop in unit prices, and thereby in total market revenue. Total profitability for the product category falls sharply, and may disappear altogether. The battle for market share continues in both existing and in yet further new distribution channels. Advertising expenditure drops to very low levels and so, eventually, does promotional expenditure. The remaining competitors make further attemps at segmentation.

Eventually manufacturers, recovering their variable cost and only part of their fixed cost, drop the product line or go out of business. Rather unpromising defensive mergers sometimes occur. Very occasionally one or two manufacturers settle in the remaining ruins to lead a spartan but not necessarily unhealthy life. Somebody still makes braces and sock-suspenders, pocket watches, cocoa powder and pipe tobacco. More rarely still, such ardent hangers-on may be lucky. Candles have been given a new lease of life (they are no longer used for lighting, but for creating an atmosphere of semi-darkness) quite apart from artificial booms caused by power cuts. Enamel kitchenware and cast-iron stoves are making a comeback. The nostalgia market is booming.

DISTORTIONS

It is to be emphasized again that the above description and the figure on page 159 summarizing it are based on the supposition that all players in the marketplace continue to stick to their original tune. (I have already implied that the main purpose of the life-cycle concept is to persuade marketers to *change* their tune when the need to do so becomes foreseeable). When the players in the marketplace do make drastic changes in their marketing, the glib picture I have described is distorted – distorted, it is to be hoped, in favour of the change-maker.

However, changes also occur outside the marketplace and some of those can have distorting effects upon the marketplace and upon the life-cycle picture that has been painted. A change in excise-duty levels distorts the trend in the beer market, the explosive spread of the Aids disease is distorting the contraceptives market, a coffee-crop failure distorts not only the coffee market but that of tea and other beverages as well, and the active commercialization of products based on new technologies will hasten the decline of markets for products based on traditional technologies.

Despite such distortions, the product life-cycle model has been used successfully in planning procedures by marketers of consumer and industrial goods and services.

CONCEPT NOT ONLY APPLICABLE TO PRODUCTS

The product life-cycle concept has been used in forecasting things like home-ownership of certain durables, the number of retail stores with scanner facilities and the profitability of door-to-door selling. Neither is the use of the concept confined to consumer products. M. T. Cunningham shows interesting examples of its use for industrial products.

STRATEGIC IMPLICATIONS

The following are a few examples of the strategic implications of all this:

1. When an originator company begins to experience accelerating sales growth of its new product (or when success is indicated in a test marketing situation), an insight into the life-cycle theory makes it imperative that a pricing strategy is determined. Is the company going to fend off competitive entries by a low price level for its product in an attempt to maintain a maximum market share for as long as possible, or will it aim for a high price level, thus inviting competitive entries and stimulating the total growth rate for the product group as a whole?

2. On the assumption that a company can assess the lead time for product improvements or for new product introductions, the use of the life-cycle concept can help to plan innovations by acting as an early-warning system for declining profits on existing products.

3. Some of the defensive mergers between companies with all their products in the maturity and decline phases would not occur if the prospective partners were fully aware of the stage of life of the other's products. Governments might not give investment grants or other forms of aid to industries if they knew that by so doing they were merely aggravating the impact of inevitable obsolescence.

FACTORS

If the product life-cycle concept, as is sometimes suggested, merely referred to sales volume, profits and unit price, then its practical use would be questionable indeed. There are, as I have already indicated, quite a number of other characteristics in the 'behaviour' of products in markets which show significant trends.

If these other characteristics can be identified and measured, then all we need to learn is how to correlate those trends and what inference can be drawn as to the expected profitability of the product in question. The state of the art has not evolved this far yet. Although quite a lot of data are collected relative to products' performance and behaviour in the marketplace, very little has been done to construct models to act as profit-forecasting tools.

The factors which, I believe, are characteristic of the stage of life products are in, and which consequently are potential indicators of a product's profit performance are the following:

1. Market penetration

Penetration is the ratio of regular buyers to the number of people to whom the product is of potential interest. For most products there is little problem in measuring penetration. There are various continuous or repetitive marketing-research services that measure penetration in any degree of detail required.

2. Distribution

Distribution is the ratio of the number of stores selling the product to those that could be potentially handling it.

There is no problem in finding out how many grocers or garages carry item X or item Y out of all grocers or all garages respectively. The problem is to determine how many stores from each trade channel are potential sellers of the product. The complexity of this problem increases every day (as anyone who realizes how a few years back grocers did not sell stockings, garden centres did not sell chocolates and garages did not sell snacks, will appreciate).

3. Consumer typology

Is there one group of people that tends to buy the product and another that does not, and, if so, what are the attitudes towards the product of each group? It is changes in these attitudes that are relevant to our purpose. I do not believe in attempts that have been made from time to time to identify 'early adopters' as such. I do not believe such people as universal 'early adopters' for all types of products exist. Whereas there may be a category of people who rarely display a pioneer attitude towards new products of any kind, most consumers will be quick to buy new products in some cases and slow in others.

4. Product function

It was the Japanese market researcher Kazuaki Ushikubo who observed that new products with low market penetration could be, and frequently are, positioned to fulfil psychological rather than purely rational functions for consumers. But, as its market share grows, the same product over time will go from being status-enhancing, exclusive (and expensive) to being ordinary, rational and cheap. A product will never move in the opposite direction. Products go down the social ladder, not up it. The inference is that if a marketer wants to hang on to his original, exclusive, high priced market segment, he will have to provide new symolic functions in his product to maintain the interest of consumers there and he must resist pressure to broaden the product's appeal.

5. Ratio of first to replacement and second-unit purchases

The usefulness for our purpose is obvious, its measurement no problem. It is quite possible that the development of the market for second (or subsequent) items in the household will prove to be, to the alert life-cyclist, quite a new market in the marketing sense (think of radios and motor cars), and should be treated as such.

6. Product proliferation

The number of varieties, sizes, applications, (optional) extras, colours, flavours, combinations – in short, the proliferation in which a product is offered – usually increases in all but the last stages of its life. Monitoring this development is an easy matter.

7. Product differentiation

This must not be confused with the previous symptom, product proliferation. Product differentiation refers to the qualitative and technological differences between products as offered by the various competing suppliers. Early on in the life of products differences tend to be greater than subsequently. Suppliers are experimenting with formulae and processes, establishing the basic physical properties of the product.

Motor cars offer an interesting illustration of both the proliferation and the differentiation symptoms: proliferation of models, colours, extras, power-packs, today is greater than ever. Differentiation (say, between manufacturer A's 4-cylinder family saloon and manufacturer B's 4-cylinder family saloon) has been reduced substantially compared with, say, 20 years ago. In most cases changes in the degree of differentiation (for that is what is relevant in our context) are not difficult to establish.

8. Number of competing brands

The number of competing brands, and increases or decreases in that number, changes in the 'cost of entry' into the market, the pattern of market shares and the change in the (combined) share of the market leader(s), all relate to the stage in the relevant product's life. Similarly the incidence of private labelling, and the growth and, later, the drop in combined private label market share, should be taken into consideration. Measurement of these characteristics by conventional methods should be no problem.

9. Advertising and sales promotion

The proportion of expenditure on theme advertising, on merchandising, on sales promotion, and the proportion of the total budget spent on activities to obtain product sampling, tell us something about the stage in the product's life-cycle. So does the total expenditure for advertising and sales promotion, as well as total expenditure per unit of sale.

The general adoption of advertising platforms explaining product properties or applications is clearly indicative of the introductory or early growth phase of a product, just as the battle of competitive claims heralds maturity. The decline phase, in as much as there are any suppliers left with enough courage and money, will show segment-orientated advertising.

It is in these last areas in particular that careful analysis of what goes on over time can help one foresee what changes in the mix and the usage of marketing tools is likely to be needed in the near future. Fortunately for quite a number of products there are good sources of advertising expenditure data. This is not quite the case for 'below-the-line' expenditure, where a proper assessment can be quite tricky.

10. Price fluctuations

Unit prices will tend to come down fairly sharply during the introductory and early-growth stages, levelling out as growth continues and early maturity is reached. A further sharp drop during late maturity and early decline is quite possible. In addition to this general trend, unit price fluctuations can occur during the early-growth stage. During the introductory and early-growth phases quite substantial unit price differentiation is very likely to occur. Observation of these phenomena should be simple.

I am not at all sure that the above is anything like a complete inventory of symptoms that surround the lives of products in markets. They are only the ones that I (and a few others) have recognized. Put down in a very rough and very generalized way, they are as shown in Table 12.1.

TABLE 12.1 Simplified characterization of life-cycle

	Introduction	Rapid growth	Maturity	Decline
Market penetration	low, early adopters	sharp increase	reaches peak	descreasing
Distribution	low, usually single 'branch'	sharp increase, mainly single 'branch'	saturation in original channel, new types of outlets discovered	remains high initially, but attrition follows
Consumer typology	homogeneous group of deliberate users	increasingly heterogeneous, some turnover, segmentation starting	segmentation reaches peak, high turnover	elderly and traditional
Product function	symbolic functions predominate	symbolic functions begin to be replaced by rational ones	symbolic functions now secondary	rational functions only
First/replacement/ second unit	first	first, replacement starting	replacement and second unit gaining on first unit	replacement mainly, some second unit
Differentiation	considerable	reducing	low	low
Proliferation	none	beginning	reaches peak	decreasing
Unit price	high	sharp drop	levelling	further drop
Pricing characteristics	differentation	some differentiation and fluctuation	very stable	defensive, protection sought
Number of brands	one or few	rapid increase	few new entries, sifting	rapidly decreasing
Share of brand leaders	unstable	fluctuations	increasing	increasing

	Introduction	Rapid growth	Maturity	Decline
Incidence of private labelling	none	rapid increase	further increase to levelling out	rapid decrease
Share of private labels	none	building up	increasing, reaches peak	dropping rapidly
Total advertising and promotion expediture	high per unit	decreasing per unit, rapid increase in total	per unit fairly stable, total still increasing but levelling later	sharp decrease
Ratio of advertising to promotion	high	decreasing gradually	further decrease	decreasing to little or nothing
Advertising and promotion theme	aimed at product awareness and applications	aimed at strong sampling effect	brand claims, dealer promotions	price promotions, attempts at segment orientation

CONCLUSION

In what I have termed the symptoms that signify the stages of a product's life in the market there is much that can be measured and evaluated. A lot is already being measured in the case of many products. There are a few facets that defy today's research technology, but there is hope for the future. Already therefore there is a lot of building material for the construction of product life-cycle models.

QUESTIONS

1. With the factors enumerated in this chapter, endeavour to determine the stage in the life-cycle of your company's main products. Does the portfolio as a whole have a bias one way or the other? If so, what does that signify?

2. As it would be useful to predict the phase in the life-cycle at which either rejuvenation programmes must be available or replacement products must have started to contribute to company net profit – the onset of 'Maturity' in fact – consider which factors in your business operations could be analysed to contribute to such a prediction.

3. How, using the product life-cycle, would you construct a case for diverting money away from an investment in plant towards an investment in product development?

13

Creativity – the Dormant Attribute

At 0513 on the 18th April 1906 a cow was standing somewhere between the main barn and the milking shed on the Old Shafter Ranch in California, minding her own business.

Suddenly, the earth shook, the skies trembled, and when it was all over, there was nothing showing of the cow above ground but a bit of her tail . . . If we do not learn to understand and guide the great forces of change at work in our world today, we may find ourselves like the Shafter cow, swallowed up by vast upheavals in our way of life – quite early some morning.

Don Fabun: *The Dynamics of Change*

OUR INTOLERANT CULTURE

It is not unreasonable, after chapters devoted to change and innovation, to look a little more closely at that mysterious attribute creativity. Bringing about the 'new' inevitably requires creativity. The people who read this book have a responsibility for being creative and for stimulating others to be creative. Without innovation there is no survival in business (or in life, for that matter), and it is first and foremost to the preoccupations of marketing that one justifiably looks as a source of innovation.

Our culture has a funny way of allocating its designation of creativity. We draw a distinction between those that are obviously expected to be creative and the rest of us (about whose creative performance we appear unconcerned). 'Creative' is applied to painters, poets, musicians, writers, sculptors, architects and designers. The rest of us by default are not. We seem in other words ready to allocate the label 'creative' to those who get paid (or at least who seek payment) for being it and withhold it from those who don't.

By taking that attitude we commit an injustice. It is an injustice not

[173]

so much because some of those we call creative are not but because most of those we do not call creative are.

Our culture is intolerant of creativity. As young people grow up, we encourage conformity, barely tolerate thought and frown upon originality. Children are taught the rules, mores and standards to abide by – which is good. But they are also taught, if by implication, that there is no need to stretch the mind beyond those rules, mores and standards. Just to make sure that children get the message, we put them in classrooms and football teams and give them uniforms to wear.

Much of this early sterilization of the mind stays with people as they grow up, and its effect becomes part of their working lifemanship. People that go into business are no exception. They do not offer and are not asked about their creative abilities. Rather, they are given job descriptions, organization charts and policy manuals and told to perform tasks, use skills or apply their knowledge of rules. The man who is mulling over the best creative idea his company ever got near to and sits staring out of the window as he does so is told to get back to work.

In addition, there are other obstacles to the emergence of creative ideas in business. The not-invented-here symptom exists not only between the company and the outside world but also between departments within the company and between people within the department. Playing it safe is a recipe applied by many people in business in the pursuit of their careers – many of them find it works. Innovation is not for those who play it safe. One way to avoid the undoubtedly high risks of innovation is to avoid innovation itself. Exponents of this school of thought will scrape the barrel of their existing business activities till the walls of the barrel wear through. In many businesses – the bigger they are, the more this is the case – authorization for changes has to be given by higher levels of management than where the idea for changes originated; then, as requests for authorization move up and subsequently down the hierarchy, the original idea stands a very good chance of being quashed, replaced or mutilated, as few managers are capable of acting as champions for the ideas of their subordinates. Pure, personal envy and fear are other obstacles to the movement of innovative ideas upwards in a managerial hierarchy.

Yet there are not many business left which have not become aware of the need to replace old products and old ways of doing things, or that have not discovered that it has become a matter of dire commercial necessity to present a discernible identity to its various publics. The business community, in other words, is now receptive to the idea that creative input into businesses is inescapable. Most business people

Just to make sure they get the message, we give them uniforms to wear.

would not dispute that marketing-based innovation has become indispensable, that uniqueness in the marketplace constitutes a more desirable aim than ever before or that the building of an unambiguous company (and brand) 'personality' is a condition for survival among its multifarious and ever more demanding publics. It is a fair guess that these people would agree that these creativity-demanding things have become vital ingredients in a company's competitiveness.

So what do companies do to get these unique-making qualities, that unambiguous personality, those crucial innovations, those vital ingredients for their competitiveness, indeed for their survival? They go and buy them outside!

Creativity is not something companies consider it worthwhile developing in-house. (Yes, there are exceptions.) Companies consider it quite in order to make (usually irreversible and very large) investments in stocks, plant, buildings and debtors, limited as the contribution to the uniqueness, innovativeness or competitiveness of those investments usually is. The idea of investing in creative ability and skills within the company itself does not arise. The company culture does not allow for creative people within its own walls, and so, despite the fact that the creative input forms the very heart and soul of the business, creative input is ordered from outside.

For designers, product-development consultants, architects, copywriters and PR consultants it is OK to be creative, provided they do it well away from the company which buys the creativity. In fact the creative people do not even meet the company people, for an 'account executive' is interposed to soften the blow. So extreme is the divide between business managers and creative people that the former have great difficulty or find it impossible to brief the latter intelligibly. These scathing comments and the slight exaggeration imply that I believe the segregation between creative and all other people is unnecessary and undesirable.

Creative ability is more developed in creative people. Creative people have learnt the disciplines of producing creative work. Creative people have the craftmanship required for their tasks. People doing creative jobs may have more creative talent than people who are not doing specifically creative jobs. But it is wrong to suggest that people on whose creative talents no demands are made are incapable of being creative. There is creative potential in most people, but it will remain snoringly dormant unless it is challenged.

I can think of no tasks or responsibility in the very broad area of marketing which can be successfully realized without creativity or that would not benefit immeasurably from the activation, development and challenging of the creative abilities of those engaged in them. Despite the total neglect (since the day they were born) of the creative capabilities of people in business, I do not think the problem of developing those capabilities is unsurmountable. Indeed help can be had (from outsiders, of course!) in setting up such development processes in a company. What is much more difficult and needs to precede any conscious effort to develop people's creative abilities is the change in the culture of a company. This can only be triggered by a determined and consistent change in attitude promulgated from the top of the organization.

WHAT IS CREATIVITY, ANYWAY?

There are bound to be quite sagacious definitions of creativity which, through ignorance of them, I am unable to quote. I make do with creativity as 'the ability to combine observations, facts or judgements in ways they have not been combined previously into a concept which is capable of being communicated'.

The particular relevance of that description stems from the implied suggestion that creativity is enhanced by an increased exposure to observations, fact and judgements. The greater this exposure, the greater the chance of coming up with new (creative) solutions. Creativity does not usually arise from sustained periods of solitary confinement in a backroom. Creativity feeds on impressions and exchanges with other people. Creative people move around and mix with other people. In business, creativeness feeds on exposure to group discussions, research findings, multi-disciplinary discussions, the media, talks with shopkeepers, housewives, spectacle wearers or decorators.

When you ask* creative people (here meant in the narrow sense, i.e. as applying to those who are actually employed to create things or ideas) what they actually do to generate creative ideas or to get creative thinking under way, they frequently tell you that they deliberately expose themselves to impressions, ideas, facts or situations in their environment. The ways of achieving that exposure vary widely, but the effect is the same.

* From *Campaign*.

Paul Leeves, Creative Director of Boase, Massimi Pollitt, says: 'It's all about dusty cupboards. You just have to have a dusty cupboard mind and, somehow, it turns into originality. I believe the best advertising is borrowing – from anywhere'.

Axel Chaldeçott, Creative Director of Wright, Collins, Rutherford Scott, says: 'I would advise him to surround himself with as much information as possible. Your mind is constantly sifting through information and juxtaposing one bit with another'.

Neil Patterson, Creative Director of Young and Rubicam, likens his mind to a fuel tank: 'I just try to keep my tank filled up all the time. I watch things, read books . . . It's all filed away because anything could be relevant for some product at some time'.

What applies to 'professional' creative people applies to the creativity of ordinary mortals as well. The brightest ideas are not going to come from people, alone, sitting behind their own desks, but from people exposed to a cacophony of impressions and from (structured) meetings of groups of very diverse people in unfamiliar circumstances.

Creativity is available, it is badly needed and it is free. If we can rid ourselves of the belief that it is important to know who generated any particular creative idea, we will have gone a long way towards exploiting the vast reserve of untapped creativity *within* the company. As David Bernstein put it: 'A good idea doesn't mind who has it'.

QUESTIONS

1. Assuming that you would feel inclined to devise ways to stimulate the creative abilities of those in your business for whose performance you are responsible, how would you ensure (a) that your people get a hearing, (b) that they get feedback and (c) that they are able to follow up whatever implications their ideas may have?

2. Chapter 4, on The Marketing Mix, distinguishes between 'hard' and 'soft' mix ingredients. Can you think of practical ways in which to shift the emphasis, if only a little, from hard to soft?

3. Try to trace which seemingly bright ideas in your company in recent times have been quashed, how that has been done and why. Can you devise a way of preventing a similar blockage on future occasions?

4. If it is true that creativity feeds on information and impressions from a multitude of sources (it is!), can you identify sources access to which would be of help?

14

The Hierarchy of Choices

Ours is a very simple policy, and we Midwesterners need simplicity. It says 20% return on equity and not a goddam thing about anything else.

Charles M. Harper, Executive Chairman of Conagra, as quoted in *Fortune*

MAKING THE FUTURE TODAY

This chapter is about how and why the future of a company is made today. It concerns thinking ahead.

There are major obstacles to thinking ahead and it is as well to recognize them, otherwise nothing can be done to surmount them:

1. The need to fight fires always elbows itself in ahead of and often replaces the need to think ahead. Today's problems are all-absorbing. If today's fires aren't fought, the house burns down. If, today, thought about the future is postponed, it will have repercussions, but not today.

2. Nothing about the future is certain, except that it will be different from today. This means that the future holds no facts and has to be assessed in terms of guesses, judgements, projections, probabilities, speculation and assumptions. Many managers feel uncomfortable with such a quicksand of uncertainty and prefer to seek refuge in the cosy certainties of today and in the irrefutable numbers of yesterday.

The reasons why it is necessary to think ahead are quite simple:

● The inevitable changes in the business environment make it imperative to change the company so as to avoid the risks and exploit the opportunities which change will put the company's way.

[181]

- Opportunities, if they remain undiscovered and are not responded to, have a nasty habit of maturing into problems. Ask yourself how many of today's problems, had you known about them when their seeds were sown, you could have either exploited or circumvented. Thought now saves panic tomorrow.

- If you make a design for the future and ensure that people know about it, the whole company and every individual in it will know where it is going. Everybody pulls in the same direction, and much of everyone's tasks and choices emerges logically from that design. The need for repeated discussion and argument every time something new crops up is thereby greatly reduced. You save large amounts of time and energy.

- Perhaps the most important result of working to a design for the future of the company is that it goes a long way towards preventing fires – thus reducing the appalling waste in time, energy and working harmony spent in firefighting.

THINKING ROUTINE

Everything in this chapter is based on an elementary thinking routine which goes something like this:

1. You decide what exactly it is you want to achieve.

2. You ensure that that aim is entirely reasonable – if it isn't you change it till it is.

3. You work out how you reckon to realize your aims.

4. You proceed along those lines, ensuring you don't get off the rails. If you do fall off, you get back on again.

PLANNING VERSUS FORECASTING

Two words that crop up frequently are forecasting and planning. There is a vast difference between the two and it is essential to understand the difference:

(a)   Forecasting is what you think is going to happen.

(b)   Planning is what you want to happen.

Planning has as its purpose to change the company so as best to meet the threats and opportunities of the future. Forecasting is what we do to reflect what we think will happen in the company's operating environment. Forecasting is also what we think will happen to the company's performance if nothing is changed in the way it operates.

THE HIERARCHY

The word 'hierarchy' was chosen in the title of this chapter to indicate that there are a number of distinct levels at which a company's pre-occupation with its future should take place. Each level has its own dimensions in the time-span, the scope, the required accuracy and the detail with which it is concerned. At each successive level the time-span shortens, the scope narrows, but the required accuracy and amount of detail increase. Each successive level takes its 'brief' from the preceding level and addresses itself to a part of its scope. For these reasons, the order in which these levels are tackled is mandatory – hence the choice of the word 'hierarchy'. Deviation from that order would result in a monumental mess.

To those who are not intimately familiar with the way management of business works in practice, the process comes across as 'taking decisions'. In TV programmes and films managers are depicted as mean-looking men who shout such things as 'Yes', 'No', 'be Goddam quick about it', and 'Make Smith and Brown do it' down one of many telephones on their desk. As the reader knows, the real world is quite different. Managers spend the greater part of their time putting out fires. If any time is left, most of that is spent trying to find out what it is that decisions need to be taken about and how and where on earth to find any half reasonable information on which to base those decisions. A further bit of time is taken to justify the postponement or avoidance of decisions. Finally, a miniscule proportion of managers' time is devoted to actual decision-taking.

This chapter, indeed this book, argues that thinking about the future is by far the most productive pursuit for managers and that managers at *all* levels should devote time and ingenuity to it. If the description

The real world is quite different . . . a miniscule part of managers' time is devoted to actual decision taking.

decision-taking is inappropriate for the way managers run the business of today, it is even more so when they plan the business of tomorrow. It is for that reason that I prefer the phrase 'making choices' and use 'Choices' in the title of this chapter.

The hierarchy of choices has the following levels:

1.   Setting of objectives and identification of (any) missions.

2.   Formulating policy.

3.   Determining strategy.

4.   Planning.

5.   Monitoring and taking corrective action.

1. Objectives and missions set out why the business exists at all. These choices are made by the owners of the business for themselves. The objectives of the business and any mission the owners may choose to impose on it constitute the task set by the owners to the management of the business. The objectives and missions will tend to be permanent.

2. Policy expresses what kind of business the management chooses to build in order to execute the tasks before it. The policy will indicate what kind of resources the company will need to acquire and develop. Conversely, of course it is the resources which a company has which have an important influence on the policy chosen. Given the interrelation of policy and resources, and because changes in resources or the development of new resources cannot be accomplished quickly, policy tends to be long-term. But policy is not forever and changes in policy must be possible even if they take years to implement.

3. Strategy, put crudely, is policy with numbers on. Strategy takes the business directions and resource requirements from the formulated policy, quantifies them and relates them to time, but it does so only in broad terms – too broad for operational decision-taking.

4. Planning specifies the strategic entities so that they become operational tasks. Both strategy-making and planning are on-going preoccupations even if time-spans are always set for both (ranging from a few years down to a few months).

5. Monitoring is simply the measurement of actual performance against expected (planned) performance, and making adjustments to

the actual performance where necessary. Monitoring is a daily concern.

Let us try and illustrate, with examples, the kind of matter which would be dealt with in each 'layer' of the hierarchy.

1. Objectives and mission

The primary objective might be formulated thus: To earn, in perpetuity, after-tax profits which, when expressed as a percentage of equity value, will be at least 2 per cent higher than the average for the engineering companies aggregated in the Dow-Jones Index.*

There are all kinds of constraints upon such an objective, not least the ever-broadening stream of laws and regulations descending upon companies from local, national and international legislative bodies. Implicit constraints are imposed, for example, by the general public on the way the company affects its environment and by labour organizations on how the company treats its employees. Constraints of this nature become explicit only if the company shows any hesitation in complying with them.

Shareholders may decide to impose additional constraints. They may choose, for example to charge the company with a mission to support or provide educational facilities in the company's local community. Shareholders may see it as a mission for the company not to have in its employ a lower proportion of particular minority groupings than occur in the national population.

Most constraints of this kind will affect most of the functional areas of the business. Marketing will certainly be affected.

It is shareholders who decide whether or not to invest in a company. Shareholders do so on the strength of the objectives they think it is reasonable to expect the company to meet and on whether the company's actual performance does so. It is then entirely reasonable that any extra constraints upon that performance can only be imposed at the behest of shareholders.

* In John Argenti's *Practical Corporate Planning* there is a well reasoned guide to target-setting.

2. Policy

Having stated that shareholders can reasonably impose constraints upon how the business is to relate to society and its environment, I must add that they are not qualified to prescribe the nature of the business the company shall conduct or the changes in the nature of the business which may be opportune over time. These choices are firmly in the province of the management.

What I call policy is the description of what the management wants the nature of the business to be, given the objectives it is required to meet and any constraints it is required to comply with. Because the operating environment of the business changes all the time, so the nature of the business will need to change with it or, if the company is very clever, just ahead of it.

The nature of the business today is the result of policy choices that were made 3, 5 or 10 years ago, and it may well be that some of the undesirable conditions in the business today are the result of making the wrong choices then. It is also possible, and more likely, that they stem from not making choices at that time at all. The policy which the business makes today will start to affect the thinking of the people from today, but may not be realized in operational terms for years yet.

Let us look at an example of the impact of policy-making on a small boiled-sweets company. This company is suffering from the combined effects of a static, over-supplied market, competition from three giant companies, and manufacturing facilities long past their prime. Profits are in decline. Note that this situation is not uncharacteristic of a frighteningly large number of businesses everywhere. The vital (and frighteningly rare) conclusion which the management, one hopes, reaches is the following: we are heading for trouble, so we must *change* something in our business. The directions in which change may be sought are:

(a)   Change the kind of business we are in (say from consumer products to industrial services). This is hardly an appropriate route, as our boiled sweets business has no resources with which it could enter new (for us) business areas. On the face of it, this route exists in theory only.

(b)   Change the product. Perhaps there is a market segment whose particular needs we could cater for (diabetics, motorists, people with worries about tooth decay, weight-watchers) and for whose precise needs we can devise the perfect product offering (including taste, colour, and packaging). It should be possible to find a segment which is so big that a modest share in it would solve our problems but small enough not to take the fancy of any of our big competitors. This is the kind of policy followed by W. A. Baxter in soup, by Wilkin in jams and by Morgan in motor cars.

There is, in theory, the possibility of making the product so advanced that it stands out from the rest of the market and can command a premium price. In the case of boiled sweets, however, this is not a policy which springs readily to mind. What does present itself as a policy worth considering is to specialize, to become associated (or to have one's brand become associated) with a single product or a narrow product category and, if possible, to monopolize it. The Dutch Rademaker Company does this (with its coffee sweets). MacDonald did it with the Penguin biscuit sandwich and the Coca-Cola company grew to global prominence through it.

(c)   Change the product range. See if our sales force, our distribution facilities and our relations with customers cannot be more fully utilized through the addition of other products to our range. Chocolate confectionery, soft drinks, snacks or biscuits might be considered. Since it is unlikely that we will be able or willing to embark upon such extensions with our own manufacturing facilities, we need to find supplies from manufacturers in industries which have over-capacity. (There are plenty of those about.)

Our product range may be changed in accord with a market segmentation choice we have made (diabetic chocolates and biscuits added to our diabetic sweets, say) or in accord with the change in our distribution policy (a focus on the hotel trade would reduce our range, say, to pre-packs only, to which could then be added postcards, gifts and souvenirs).

(d)   Change distribution. Our current sales are, say, 70 per cent through confectionery/newsagent/tobacconist outlets, 20 per cent through grocers and 10 per cent through 'all others'. We find the competitive pressures greatest in grocers, followed by CTNs. With the enormously wide distribution of confectionery products, we might well find distribution channels where volume is large enough to accommodate our target volume of business comfortably and yet to which our big three competitors are not devoting the crushing care which they lavish on grocers and CTNs. Following this line of thought, we might well choose gradually to increase our selling effort to one or two of the other categories of outlets handling confectionery, such as variety stores, chemists, garden centres, petrol stations, vending machines, cinemas, sports stadia, bus and railway stations, air and ferry terminals, or hotels.

(e) Change sideways. If we are unhappy with the way things are going in the home market, what is to stop us going abroad? Foreign markets are well documented and we should not find it difficult to choose, say, three markets to investigate in more detail with a view to starting up in business in one of them.

Now the management of our boiled sweets company has looked at the options, it must choose which ones to take. Quite possibly it will decide on a compound policy, i.e. use more than one of the five routes indicated above. It can do so by interrelating those options or by exercising several quite separately from one another. Let us assume our management chooses as follows.

1. (Distribution). The company chooses to increase its distribution effort to service hotels and air and ferry terminals. It will also seek to enter the market, not previously identified, of international passenger carriers, i.e. ferries, international bus services, and airlines.

2. (Product). For the selected markets, the company will be able to supply only in pre-packs. Products will need to be distinctive and of above average quality. The brand used will have to have international relevance and acceptability. Packing must reflect these requirements.

3. (Product range). The product range, to be practical for the type of outlet sought, must be very narrow and distinctive. Since we wish to build a franchise with consumers in this away-from-home market, we must apply one brand to each product in the range, and the makeup of the range should encourage the customer to buy several items in it. We shall buy in what we cannot make.

4. (Moving sideways). It will take time to build the kind of business we are setting out to develop. Our existing business, meanwhile, must not only go on but must provide the funds to finance the development and the many hours that will go into the changes we have chosen to make.

Therefore, as a first priority, we shall find ways to gain sales of our existing products in foreign markets. Germany, Italy and France will be investigated to that end. We shall look for agents or distributors with whom we shall aim to make agreements linked to volume of product sold.

The changes we have decided to make in our marketing policy, however, also aim to take us abroad. International carriers will point us to air, bus and ferry terminals at the foreign point of destination and from there we shall develop business in hotels. Local suppliers will be sought as and when necessary.

So far this is an entirely fictitious illustration. It goes without saying that, when such a policy is formulated, a considerable number of tasks emerge, and it does not go without saying, but it is very much the case, that those tasks will have to be performed on an extra-curricular basis, i.e. by the people already in the company on top of what they are doing already!

The example I have given naturally focuses on marketing. But policy choices are made with regard to every aspect of the business: staffing, employee relations and training; financial management and accounting; manufacturing; engineering and purchasing.

SWOT

As was said earlier, policy-making is all about matching resources to what goes on in the business environment. Mindful of what you read in the Introduction about the use of jargon, it is with trepidation that I refer to a well worn concept known as the SWOT audit. The SWOT (Strengths, Weaknesses, Opportunities, Threats) exercise consists of trying to match up the strengths and weaknesses of your own company against the opportunities and threats you perceive in the business environment. The idea is that you assess, in each case, whether and how well you are equipped competitively to exploit opportunities, and whether you can forestall or circumvent threats and if you cannot, how you will employ your resources to overcome them.

A SWOT audit is crucial to any plans for boosting a company's competitiveness. It not only points to where resources are best applied but also to what those resources should be in the first place.

There are obvious resources, such as money (sometimes what is more obvious is the lack of it), manufacturing facilities, inventories, distribution equipment etc. Then there are the less obvious resources –

raw material/product/process know-how, market knowledge, research skills and, of course, customers.

A conscientious soul search will uncover all these resources and – more importantly – how in relation to each the company stacks up against the competition. What is extremely difficult is to discover hidden resources. A company's culture will blind it to some of its real competitive strengths (and weaknesses!). It is one thing to have strength or weakness in a particular area, but quite another thing to be aware of those strengths and weaknesses. Some readers will dismiss this observation about companies' unawareness of their own strengths as unrealistic nonsense. Yet it is true. In fact companies quite often are not only unaware of their real competitive strengths but pride themselves on attributes which have little competitive significance in the marketplace. Some examples will illustrate these points:

- The Royal Bank of Canada has been buying advertising space to tell us, 'Look to us for an imaginative approach to banking'. To most readers, one would assume, imaginativeness is not the first attribute in bankers which springs to mind, and so the Royal Bank of Canada's claim is intriguing. Immediately, however, the Bank puts its foot in it by announcing: 'Assets US $66.9 billion. Network: 1500 branches worldwide, operating units in almost 50 countries and more than 5000 correspondent relationships'. Does the Royal Bank of Canada believe that statement implies imagination? It sounds rather as if the RBC is just another big bank.

- I was called to Acmesa, a small, regionally operating dairy company which believed its strength lay in its manufacturing capability. Since its production managers had been to the same school as the production managers of most other dairy companies, since they used similar equipment and identical raw materials, the competitive edge, it seemed, was perhaps overstated. A recent piece of available consumer research was helpful in carrying out a SWOT analysis. We ended up by beefing up the company's own product-development activity, adding a whole range of products sourced outside, and setting up sales training and briefing programmes to exploit the tremendous strength the company had through its daily access to every household in its market.

- A publishing company felt that its main marketing strength lay in the excellent rapport its salesmen had with booksellers, and indeed this was a powerful asset. The company's largest and most profitable title series consisted of attractive looking, colourful hardback books sold at very reasonable prices with an unending range of titles on every conceivable spare-time pursuit. What the company hadn't realized was that with that series it had successfully built a significant stake in the gifts market. Once this realization dawned, it became possible to exend marketing activities greatly and effectively, especially in the areas of distribution and advertising.

- A radio and television broadcasting station was suffering a decline in the size of its audiences; its profitability had been affected and its very solvency was threatened. The two main programme divisions had each gone through various evaluative processes and found that programme quality was rated highly among their respective audiences. Neither the programme editors nor central management had made any attempt to assess any weaknesses in the organization's effort. Yet to find the cause of the problem proved extremely simple: almost unanimously, the audience held the view that the station suffered from having a split personality. One section of the audience was offended by the programmes liked by the other, and programmes liked by the former section were dismissed as boring by the latter. Two strong-minded programme directors working under weak central management were virtually free to shape their own wholly divergent programme strategies with the result that they were pulling the station's audience apart.

No, it is not easy for the people inside it to identify and weigh their organization's strengths and weaknesses, or at any rate to do so objectively, comprehensively and accurately. That the effort to carry out such an analysis must be made has already been argued and exemplified by the case summaries given. When attempts at analysis are made, it is useful to remember that the very existence of a business enterprise depends upon the relations between it and diverse groups of people outside it, and that therefore those groups of people are an ideal source of judgement on what the company is good and bad at.

Chapter 15 on Planning will discuss the business environment, which is where most of the opportunities and threats facing the enterprise lie. Most, but not all. Some opportunities and threats occur within the organization. A breakthrough from R & D, unexpected talents discovered in new employees, the appearance of a new kind of raw material, or new ways of utilizing manufacturing equipment are examples of opportunities that can arise within the business. Opportunities sometimes stem directly from strengths and weaknesses. For example, the broadcasting company's weakness of presenting a split personality to its audience pointed to obvious remedial action. Acmesa's strong sales and distribution facilities provided it with the opportunity to quintuple its sales and profit in just a few years.

Here is an example of an actual SWOT audit and the 'solutions' arising from it. The real-life case was more detailed and quantified than is described here, only the fundamental decisions which followed the analysis are recorded. The company concerned is a medium-sized packaged consumer goods company.

Weaknesses were identified as follows:

1. Unsteady profit history due to heavy dependence on raw materials with widely gyrating prices.

2. High debt/equity ratio. Helped by unsteady profitability, limited access to further borrowed or equity funds.

3. Low market shares in every one of many markets.

4. Attainment of low unit cost production hampered by inability to achieve long production runs (different products for different markets), and limited manufacturing know-how.

5. Localized weak patches in quality of management.

6. Little consistency of marketing strategy across the various markets served.

7. Under-funded and scattered R & D effort.

Strengths within the company were perceived to be:

1. Company truly international, selling in ninety countries, of which seven are main markets, with manufacturing facilities in six of those.

2. Some main markets very profitable.

3. Some flexibility in shifting production to most favourable areas.

4. Very good internal human relations.

5. Availability of managers with international experience.

6. Well trained sales staff in all main markets.

7. Above-average design capability and design-management experience.

Solutions were sought in three (strategic) directions:

1. To slow down or stop expansion of production capacity to meet increasing sales and gradually build up required volume by commissioning production from other manufacturers. By shifting part of the required product volume from 'make' to 'buy':

(a) Reliance on unstable raw material prices was reduced (weakness 1).

(b) Working capital requirements were reduced, resulting in reduced borrowings and improved debt/equity ratios (weakness 2).

(c) A much more flexible attitude to the composition of the sales-product range became possible. Products for which the company had neither the know-how nor the manufacturing facilities could now be sold. Conversely, the company's manufacturing facilities were now able to concentrate on products the company was best at (weaknesses 4 and 7, strength 3).

(d) By focusing on suppliers with under-utilized manufacturing facilities and/or high levels of manufacturing efficiency, it proved possible to share the benefits from these conditions with the suppliers.

(e) The skills required from people the company sent as specifiers/ controllers to its manufacturing suppliers, once initial problems had been overcome, became a valuable asset and provided an ideal training ground for young managers aspiring to the international arena (weakness 5, strength 1).

2. It was realized that the tolerance for inadequate management performance needed to be reduced. In the event the weak patches were strengthened through moving people around rather than by firing and hiring. It was learnt at the same time that the seed bed from

which international managers could be drawn needed to be extended. This was accomplished by moving more young people through junior management posts in group companies in different countries, by putting young managers on international project teams, and by specifiers/controllers developing the capability to operate internationally (weakness 5, strengths 1 and 5, solution 1(e)).

3. It is without a doubt the 'discovery' of the potential benefits from market segmentation which provided the best solution. It had an overriding impact on the future of the business. Most of the company's sales were of consumer products sold the world over under a single brand. Two vital conditions needed to be established:

(a)   Behind the internationally uniform brand there should be an internationally consistent 'personality'. The internationalizing consumer made inconsistencies in that personality unacceptable.

(b)   The 'personality' the company was seeking to establish for its brand had to be compatible with the modest share the brand had in every one of its markets. If possible, the brand had to be positioned so as to be relatively unassailable by the giants in the marketplace. Some research was available to suggest where unassailable niches were to be found. Significantly it was in or close to such niches that the brand was actually positioned in the countries where the company was the most profitable. It was therefore not difficult to define the segment the brand needed to be repositioned to serve in those countries where it wasn't doing so already.

The repositioning of a brand requires effort and resources, because you are trying to interest people who have never heard of it or people who regard the brand as inappropriate for them. The repositioning took several years to accomplish but it was achieved through:

1.   Reformulation of most products, the redesign of some products and a complete redesign of every package in the product range.

2.   Sweeping changes in pricing, distribution-channel selection, sales promotion and advertising to home in on the chosen segment.

3.   Targeting and considerably expanding the 'D' of R & D (financed from robbing the 'R' and placing it on a back

burner) and bringing about an integration of the development and design programmes.

4. Boosting the education and training of the sales force throughout the years of the repositioning programme.

The effect on the company was quite dramatic. Not only did its financial performance improve considerably, but, through the participation of many in the whole soul-searching process, the company culture changed. From a company in a state of continuous search and trial, it became, because of the SWOT exercise, a goal-directed company, since it knew where it was going.

3. Strategy

Strategy is the phase in the design of the company's future which takes the directional indications from policy towards tasks to be accomplished by the operational sectors of the business. Earlier I called strategy 'policy with numbers on' related to time, and that it certainly is – and more. Not only does it say, 'We want to go so far in the given direction in 3 years' time and we need so much of such and such resources to do it', strategy will also concern itself with the 'how' of achieving those goals if the how is significantly different from the company's experience to date.

To go back to our sweets company, the policy statement has prescribed the markets it wants to develop business in, and gives directions regarding the products required for those markets. The strategic statement will give a target volume of business to be achieved. It will in fact give minimum and maximum values for sales, cost and expenses, but it will also go into 'how' by indicating which resources are to be fielded. It might even go into the question of which resources are expected to be generated within the business (say training/recruiting salesmen, formulating new products) and which will need to be obtained outside (say securing supplementary products, making arrangements with contract packers and distributors, engaging product development and design consultancies for our new products).

The strategic plan should culminate in numbers, such as profit in pounds sterling, to reflect whether the company is on a course to achieving its objectives as set by the company's shareholders.

4. Planning

Planning details strategy so as to make it operationally task-setting for all levels of management. In that respect the difference between strategy and planning is one of degree only, and quibbling about which term covers which could be justifiably dubbed as hair-splitting. I have deliberately, under the previous heading, used the term 'strategic plan', but I have not done so mainly to confuse the reader. Planning as understood in this book sets out what operations are expecting to achieve during some specific future period: for example, how much of which product manufacturing is to produce, what production facilities engineering is expected to make available, what materials (raw and otherwise) purchasing is expected to procure, and of course how much of which product sales is expected to sell.

Strategic choices go beyond these operational concerns to such questions as whether we made or buy, whether we build a business or acquire a company already in it, or whether we develop skills inside the business or go outside for them.

5. Monitoring

This final phase belongs in the hierarchy because of Murphy's Law: 'If you have done everything possible to ensure nothing can go wrong, something will!' If something goes wrong, you are faced with such choices as 'Do I put it right this evening or will tomorrow do?' 'Do we tell the customer we're sorry or do we ask the guys to work overtime', or 'Do we ship the batch or do we not ship the batch, or do we ship the batch and tell them about the missing spanner?' Failure to monitor or failure to act swiftly and decisively upon feedback from the monitoring job has resulted in some of the most catastrophic of business disasters. Not infrequently the discoveries from a monitoring job become major inputs for subsequent policy-making.

WHO DOES WHAT?

In describing the 'hierarchy of choices' the way I have done, I do not want to create the impression that in a company – and I mean in a company of any size, right to the biggest you can think of – you have a

. . . do we tell them about the missing spanner?

bunch of people who make policy, a different bunch who make strategy, a third bunch to do the planning, and then, finally, a fourth bunch who run the business. If 20 years ago in some big companies you had a situation which was a little bit like that, I won't argue. But that was 20 years ago; it is not so now.

When we were talking about objectives and a mission, I said that shareholders set an objective and impose missions on a company. If you have a situation – as in many non-English-speaking countries – where you have two boards, one to represent the interests of share-holders and a second one to run the business, and where the law provides for the possibility of the former bossing the latter, then you have a forum where shareholders talk to managers. In British or American companies you have nothing other than shareholders' meetings, where it is regrettable that such matters are so rarely discussed. By and large, shareholders vote when they telephone who-ever it is that does their stock buying and selling for them.

It has been argued that the choices a company makes about its future, all the way up and down the hierarchy, are choices that everyone in the organization should know about and act in accordance with. And contribute to?

Let us tackle the first argument first. The disparate natures of indi-viduals who together form a company make it imperative that each is thoroughly conversant with their companies' aims, mores, mission, policy, strategy and plans. How else can they act in accord with common goals, in harmony with each other. How else can their actions be compatible and consistent?

Fresh out of university, ignorant and inquisitive as such places make you, I worked for a company at whose managing director I used to fire my many questions about why we did, or did not, do certain things a certain way. Frequently his answer would be: 'I cannot discuss that with you; it is a matter of policy'. I made two discoveries. The first was unimportant: the phrase was my managing director's way of saying 'I don't know'. The second discovery was that my managing director was of the view that (a) policy was something determined in the smoke-laden atmosphere of the boardroom and (b) it was not for communication to those in the business who were not party to the goings-on in the boardroom.

The breed to which my managing director belonged may not be dying out, but mercifully fewer of that breed nowadays make it to managing director. The *very purpose* of the choices made in the whole of the hierarchy is that they become part of the thinking and doing of every soul in the company.

How else can they act in accord with common goals, in harmony with each other?

So much for 'knowing about' and 'acting in accordance with' objectives, policy, strategy and plans. What about 'contributing to'?

The answer is 'yes'. A company should be run so that anyone in it can make contributions to policy, strategy and plans. When discussing the role of monitoring, I pointed out that from it very substantial contributions to the shaping of policy (and what follows) can emerge. (In companies making motor cars, margarine, bridges and pharmaceuticals this circumstance will be engraved on people's minds!)

There are three dimensions by which a man in the organization should be able and encouraged to contribute to all or any levels of destiny-making. The first is that he contributes to whatever level of management immediately affects his own operating environment. A machine operator might contribute to engineering planning, or a subsidiary company manager might contribute to acquisition strategy. The second is that a man, through the managerial hierarchy, should be able to contribute to any level in the 'hierarchy of choices'. The third is that the company might consider setting up project teams with a deliberately chosen diverse group of people from all strata and functional areas to think about and discuss policy. The two main reasons why active and intensive participation of many in the organization will prove to be highly beneficial are that there are almost certainly some good ideas out there. Participation in these matters is the most powerful motivator of people you could devise.

QUESTIONS

1. Can you think of recent major problems in your business which could have been either circumvented or exploited as opportunities had you had the appropriate knowledge earlier?

2. '. . . it may well be that some of the undesirable conditions in the business today are the result of making the wrong choices then (i.e. 3, 5 or 10 years go). It is also possible, and more likely, that they stem from not making choices at that time at all.' Where does your business stand?

3. Carrying out a SWOT analysis frequently reveals Ss, Ws, Os and Ts which had not previously been identified. Where this has been the case, are you able to trace the process by which this discovery was made? If so, could a transposition of that process

to different parts of the business not lead to other valuable discoveries?

4. Have deliberate searches among the various groups of stakeholders been conducted to identify their perceptions of the company's strengths and weaknesses? Are such searches repeated at regular intervals?

15

Planning Is Not Dead

You can never plan the future by the past.

Edmund Burke in a letter to a member of the
National Assembly

NO PLANNERS?

In the previous chapter about destiny-shaping you did not read anything about *planners*. The reason is that the whole process described
here has become too important to be left to planners. Policy formulation, strategy-making and planning* have become much more
difficult as discontinuities increasingly dominate the business environment. It is unfortunate that the more difficult it is to look ahead in
time, the more essential it is to do so. Conversely, but no longer of any
practical significance, the easier it is to plan ahead, the less urgency
there is to do it.

Policy, strategy and plans are now firmly the responsibility of managers. There is now constant pressure on companies to innovate pro-
actively, to act speedily, to be more flexible, to work with reduced
pay-back periods, and to consider and respond to the needs and
attitudes of people other than customers and shareholders. Given this
pressure, it can only be the managers themselves who can take the
responsibility for and, with luck and determination, develop some
measure of ability in deciding where the business wants to go and how
it intends to get there.

It is not a bad idea to have a man in the organization who co-
ordinates and administers the entire planning process – a man,

* Some people use the term 'planning' or 'strategic planning' for these three things
lumped together. I believe that their separation lent clarity to the process.

[203]

moreover, who can chase managers up and who can ask awkward questions about omissions, ambiguities and inconsistencies in what managers have come up with. To call him 'planner' is OK by me – as long as managers carry the can.

THE REVOLUTION IN PLANNING

In what follows under this heading the term 'planning' will be used, wherever applicable, to include policy formulation and strategy-making, since the 'revolution' took place in all three areas and it is convenient to use a single word.

It was in the 1960s that planning came into widespread use in European business. Then in or around 1974 a number of events drastically altered companies' approach to planning. I do not think 'revolution' is too strong a term to describe what happened. A good way to demonstrate the vital importance of planning in today's management of a business is to look at what happened after 1974 and why it happened.

Changes in planning practice were not made for the fun of it. There were very compelling reasons. I will summarize them.

1 January 1974: Discontinuity

Give or take a few months, on 1 January 1974 there were some very dramatic events, and these were rapidly followed by other dramatic, mainly unconnected, events:

1. Exploding energy prices, followed by a shift in the distribution of energy sources.

2. Mainly growing and erratic inflation rates.

3. Widening and increasingly erratic currency exchange rates.

4. Stagnating economic growth rates and decline.

5. Soaring cost of money.

6. Virtual doubling of wage costs in N. Europe – now the highest in the world.

7. Rapid internationalization of competition.

8. Mushrooming local, regional, national and international government intervention.

9. Growing politicalization of customers, especially those in newly industrializing countries.

10. Growing unemployment, with its social consequences and cost.

11. Deteriorating political stability in many countries.

12. Actual or threatened scarcities of various resources other than energy (fish, agricultural crops, various minerals).

13. Spread of actual pollution and public pollution consciousness.

As these events occurred, they replaced the continuities with which all those who had been in business since the Second World War grew up.

Simplistically, but conveniently, I should like to call 1 January 1974 the 'watershed' of the planning process in companies. The advent of discontinuities in the business environment provoked various kinds of responses, each with its own effect on planning procedures. These responses may be categorized as follows:

1. The company discovers that its planning system no longer works. It stops planning altogether. It settles for a succession of panic situations which occur at every unexpected event and believes this is now the norm.

2. The company discovers that its planning system no longer works. It doesn't change the planning system except that the planning span is reduced from 10 years to 3 years.

3. The company discovers that its planning system no longer works. The company takes stock of the situation and concludes that there is no reason to stop playing the game just because the rules have been changed. The company decides to learn the new rules, and reorganizes its planning procedures.

Companies making one of the first two responses, if they survive, tend to come around to the third type of response, and since that is the only one that works, we shall examine it further.

Let me give you some examples* of companies whose planning

---

* Some of these examples were taken from a series of articles which appeared in the *Financial Times*.

procedures went through this kind of transition. Platmanifactur (PLM) of Malmo, Sweden, a packaging materials company, had successfully used strategic planning since the mid-1940s. When I say 'successfully', I mean that its planning procedures had enabled the company to take three major sets of strategic decisions between the late 1940s and late 1960s, each of which had resulted in substantial contributions to profit growth.

The first 'long-range' plan was made in the mid-1940s. Subsequent plans, each with a 10-year span, were made in 1959 and 1969. PLM had one of the largest marketing research and planning departments in Scandinavia, and the extensive surveys which underpinned the Plans covered not only the packaging field in depth but identified major social trends generally. The 1969 plan had taken 3 years to put together!

By the early 1970s it became clear that the forecasts in the 1969 plan were useless. Changes affecting the business were coming along too rapidly. So the planning system was changed drastically. Coincidentally, the company was reorganized into five fairly autonomous operating divisions and three service divisions, each a profit centre. The changes in the planning system were as follows:

1. The central marketing research and planning department was closed. 'You can no longer let staff people plan for the doers!', the company's managing director said.

2. Planning was decentralized and put under the direct responsibility of each of the divisional managers.

3. The planning span was reduced from 10 years to 6, out of which only the first 3 were expressed in monetary terms of sales, profit and investment targets. The first of these became the operating budget.

4. The planning cycle was changed from 10-year end-to-end to annual roll-over, with central management meeting at least once a month for monitoring purposes.

5. A top-down and bottom-up consultative procedure was adopted. It comprised the following main elements:

(a)   A strategic brief was drawn up between central and divisional management.

(b)   Divisional management, down to foreman level, drew up a detailed plan.

(c)   All divisional managers met with central management to draw
      up a corporate plan.

Jarl Bafving, PLM's deputy Managing Director, made a statement
which it seems relevant to quote: 'The purpose of strategic planning is
less to produce exact forecasts than to create, within the company, the
attitudes, values and behaviour which makes possible the positive
changes we want.'

At Shell the planning approach is based upon the identification of a
consistent pattern of social, economic, political and technological
development which is then incorporated into two sharply contrasting
scenarios (as planners' jargon has it) – a 'best' and 'worst' situation.
Operational managers are then expected to produce a set of plans for
their divisions to fit each of the extreme scenarios. The logic behind the
principle is that reality will end up somewhere between the extremes,
and the two alternative plans should between them be able to cope
with reality when it comes along.

The Dutch Melk Unie Holland food company decided to replace its
planning procedures. I say 'replace' because the company even
decided to drop the term 'planning' and instead chose the phrase
'corporate development'. Explaining the replacement of the word
'planning' to its divisions, the company's central management said:

(a)   The word 'planning' is too closely associated with the process of
      extrapolating from present circumstances and possibilities, in
      which events in our business environment are not adequately
      integrated.

(b)   The word 'planning' is too suggestive of accurate quantifiable
      data; it doesn't allow for uncertainties and qualitative
      approximations.

(c)   'Planning' implies a specialized activity (of the corporate planner).

'Corporate development' should be a *continuous* process in which an
attempt is made to *actualize the future* and in which process the *whole* of
the company's *management* participates.

From the companies which have made fundamental changes in
their planning procedures which the examples have sought to
illustrate, certain common features emerge. The first fundamental
change in planning practice was the basic assumption which underlies

the very future of companies. Any business manager with less than 30 years' experience at the time of the watershed knew of only one such assumption: *growth*. That assumption, quite suddenly, had to make way for a completely unfamiliar one: *discontinuity*.

Changes, the very stuff that discontinuity is made of, all begin in a small way. Small beginnings give off weak signals. For two reasons it became essential to pick up weak signals before they gained strength:

1. An awful lot of problems start life as opportunities, so if you catch a change early in its life, the chances of being able either to circumvent it or to exploit it are enhanced.

2. To gain a competitive advantage.

Planning has always aimed at reducing risks. In the days before the watershed that meant avoiding speculation. Today most managers realize that the most hazardous form of speculation is *not* to speculate. So the main characteristic of today's planning is to make assumptions, assessments, guesses, and evaluations – all very speculative stuff and deliberately so.

Given a much greater complexity of factors affecting the futures of our business and the accelerating speed at which changes are thrust upon us, surely planning must have become correspondingly complex?

No, it hasn't. It has become much simpler.

It has *had* to become simpler, and we must ensure that it remains simple, for three good reasons:

(a) Many more and quite different people in the company are now engaged in planning. They are its managers – people who have neither the inclination nor the time for complications.

(b) We need the flexibility to make changes frequently and fast. You cannot do that to complex things.

(c) When dealing with policy and strategy, we are dealing with the main issues in changing the company into what we want it to become; and main issues, blissfully, are usually simple. Only the short-term operating plans show any complexity at all.

So important is this aspect of simplicity that General Electric – one of the world's giant corporations – in its planning 'constitution' states that its (centrally triggered) planning procedure must, first, concentrate on essentials, second, insist on top management involvement, and third, avoid diffusion (of attention and effort) through concentration upon a small number of important challenges.

In pre-watershed days the plan was (almost) sacrosanct. Commitment to it was assumed and expected. Today, to paraphrase Marshall MacLuhan, 'The process is the message'. 'The numbers in the plan are far less important than the thinking behind them and the process of doing the exercise' is the attitude of a London company, Williams Lea, whose dedication to planning has helped it to realign itself completely to its markets.

The planning process 'being the message' rather than the actual plan means that the whole of the planning procedure now is designed in such a way that the result of any change in the assumptions which underlie it can be ascertained quickly (known in the trade as 'what if' systems). In pre-watershed days only a depth charge would have budged assumptions underlying a plan.

Table 15.1 summarizes the very fundamental changes in strategic planning which have come about since the watershed.

TABLE 15.1   The changes in planning – typical features

Before watershed	After watershed
Purpose: identify best growth opportunities for maximum profitability	Purpose: earliest identification of company vulnerability in quest for survival
Main task: quantify best growth opportunities	Main task: pick up weak signals
Underlying assumption: growth	Underlying assumption: discontinuity
Philosophy: seeks to reduce speculation	Philosophy: deliberately speculative
Objective: singular and profit-orientated	Objective: multiplicity of objectives, roles and missions; survival-orientated
Commitment: commitment to plan expected	Commitment: commitment to planning process expected
Assumptions: assumptions behind plan are inflexible	Assumptions: planning system designed to quickly show results whenever assumptions are changed. ('What if' systems)
Format: complex and extensive	Format: simple and brief
Main content: quantified data	Main content: assessments, evaluations, estimates, and judgements

TABLE 15.1 **The changes in planning – typical features (*contd*)**

Before watershed	After watershed
Components: high forecast component	Components: low forecast components. Predictions typically in 'best' and 'worst' extremes
Type of forecast: strongly extrapolatory, often without stated assumptions	Type of forecast: little extrapolatory element in any forecasts. Typical forecast is contingency forecast with reasoned assumptions
Input: substantial input from statistical analyst. Simulation and modelling widely used	Input: substantial input from managers and 'futurists' to give (alternative) scenario predictions
Timing: long planning time-span. Low review and revision frequency. End-to-end periodicity	Timing: short planning time-span. High review and revision frequency. Roll-over periodicity
Main thrust: given by planner	Main thrust: given by chief executive and much increased involvement of all levels of management
Organisational: planners assemble and process data and issue plan to management	Organisational: basic strategic premises established by top management in consultation with operating management. Plans drawn up by various levels of operational management. Plan consolidated in consultation between top management and operational managers

'Planning is difficult, especially when it concerns the future', some wit once remarked. That is probably as true now as it was in the early 1970s, but at least it has become more down to earth, and it has become the province of the very people that use it: managers.

QUESTIONS

1. Against what you have read in this chapter, try to identify where your company's planning procedures stand.

2. 'You can no longer let staff people plan for the doers!' Assess the validity of that statement.

3. Planning in the good old days meant reducing risks. Now planning deliberately speculates. It has to. What particular approaches to speculation about the future are taken in your company? Are there any new elements you would consider adding to this process?

4. How do you ensure that every level of management in your company participates in planning?

16

Competitiveness

1. The quality of much UK manufacturing management is low, leading to ineffective business operations.

2. Many top level manufacturing managements are insufficiently demanding and do not aim for high enough standards of achievement.

3. In many companies the management attempts to operate with insufficient information for informed and effective decision-making.

4. Substantial scope exists in many companies for improving the supply performance provided to customers.

5. Present purchasing arrangements accentuate the importance of price in comparison with other considerations.

6. An emphasis on low price is moving products undesirably 'down-market' and into small margins.

7. Although an innovative approach may suit some manufacturing companies a 'market follower' approach may be more appropriate for others.

8. Poor long term performance is likely to be a factor contributing to the poor image of UK manufacturing.

Main conclusions in the report *Competitiveness in UK Manufacturing Industry – A survey** conducted by A. R. Ovenden Management Consultants for the British Institute of Management in 1986

ATTITUDE OF MIND

In this closing chapter we look at a few aspects of competitiveness. The whole book of course is about competitiveness and suggests that, much as competition takes place in the marketplace, it has to do not

* Survey based on forty companies with sales of £2½bn from ten industries.

just with marketing but with every aspect of a company's activity by every one of its people. Competitiveness in a business cannot be achieved without a shared sense of purpose, a total orientation towards customers, the extensive use of knowledge, open communications between people in the business and a considerable measure of energy and perseverance.

Becoming competitive is not easy. Competitiveness does not arise from easy solutions, such as more investment, increased R & D, less government interference, more government subsidies, or a better agreement with the unions. Much as some (or all) of these things help, competitiveness is an attitude of mind – an attitude in the minds of everyone in the business. Attitudes, or changed attitudes, require enormous effort to bring about. That effort must be consistent, continuous and top-down in the organization.

Competitiveness among the people in a business is helped if the following conditions are established:

1. Making sure that everyone knows what the business is about in terms of the customer benefits it delivers.

2. Making sure everyone knows where the business wants to get to, encouraging maximum participation in the underlying choices, and showing frequently where the business is in relation to its targets.

3. Defining and exhibiting competitive strengths and demonstrating how these are being further enforced.

4. Setting standards as well as targets for everyone's performance, involving them in that process.

5. Ensuring that individual performance is frequently evaluated against standards and targets, immediately rewarding better than expected performance and penalizing less than expected performance. Being ruthless about wilful under-performance, carelessness or indifference.

6. Making the design of the company's future an open forum in which contributions from anyone can be harvested and, where appropriate, rewarded.

Competitiveness and competition in business suffer from a bad image, probably because they are not understood. Significantly, precisely the same competitiveness and competition are universally regarded with the greatest favour if they occur in the very desirable but socio-economically much less important area of sport. There men and women are applauded for covering themselves in mud, exposing themselves to extremes of cold and wet, suffering great discomfort and endangering life and limb.

The popular view is that competitiveness in business is socially irresponsible. It pushes out poorly performing people. Worse, poorly performing management pushes out people regardless of their performance. Competition can ruin industries or lay towns or regions to waste. In truth of course it is *un*competitiveness which brings about such social disasters.

Competitiveness generates the resources to invest in growth, not least in new jobs. Thus it builds industries and boosts the economies of towns, regions and nations. Competitiveness challenges and stimulates people. Being competitive is rewarding. There is no reason why competitiveness should rule out compassion. Competitiveness can be and should be a most humane pursuit.

WE DON'T CHOOSE OUR COMPETITORS

Our trade associations, government agencies, statistics offices, trade unions, educational system – indeed, our entire cultural environment – makes us believe our competitors are those who use the same kind of resources we use. If our raw material comes from cows' udders, we are dairy manufacturers competing with other dairy manufacturers. If we use lathes and stamping machines, we are engineers and we compete with other engineers. If we run shops that sell meat, we compete with other butchers.

But it is not our trade associations, the government or the unions who decide who our competitors are. The total authority of choosing our competitors is vested in our customers. They vote in complete freedom . . . with their purses. Customers do not know or care about our neatly administered trade associations, the diligent statisticians or the tenacious shop stewards. Customers will reward whoever offers better value for money, not whoever has more lathes or is better at stamping. Customers will buy where they find the best selection of foods, not where most dead animals hang from the ceiling. Customers showed no allegiance to the Swiss watch industry when unheard of people from Taiwan started selling accurate, cheap electronic watches.

Oil companies abandoned ships when pipeline-building technology provided cheaper and more reliable transport. Pupils' love of books will crumble under the impact of new, cheap and versatile electronic carriers of knowledge in teaching communications.

True, suppliers, mostly those we have never heard of or thought about, will trigger new thoughts and ideas among our existing customers. But it is they – the customers – who will select our competitors for us.

This is why companies have to express their role among their customers in terms of the sort of benefits they deliver and not in terms of raw materials used, processes applied, skills used or the locations at which they manufacture. To remain competitive, companies need to know everything about the way customers perceive the benefits inherent in their product offering and how those benefits may be increased.

Customers' behaviour changes all the time. It changes, as this book is at pains to point out, at an ever increasing pace. This means that if we, as a company, or our brand or our product wish to remain the *same* (best, modern, efficient, convenient, fast, comfortable or whatever), we must change with our customers' perceptions of whatever is best, most modern, efficient, convenient, fast or comfortable. In order to retain the *same* perceived attributes we have to *change* our product offering all the time. Motor car brands illustrate the trend. (*Some* motor car brands illustrate the trend, that is!)

GLOBAL MARKETS

One of the great benefits bestowed upon those of the world's customers who have the means to buy things is the tremendous decline in the real cost of transport. To give an example of what this has led to today, food shops in the 'developed' countries will commonly display products from dozens of nations. In Europe we import vast quantities of fresh foods from the Antipodes and from Europe we are now able profitably to supply such mundane items as bread and water across the Atlantic.

Similar situations arise in most product fields and an increasing number of services markets. The inevitable conclusion is that few suppliers can escape international competition, and many experience global competition even when they confine their marketing activities to their home market.

NO CONFINES

So both competition confined to a single technology and competiton confined to a single national market are losing out. Neither technological nor geographic parameters can be relied upon any longer to offer protection against competitive attacks from outsiders. In the pursuit of competitiveness only the extending and strengthening of customer benefits have relevance, and far broader technological and geographic areas will need to be scanned to find opportunities and solutions. This strategic caveat is illustrated by my example in Chapter 6, which suggests that some three-quarters of the new food products to come to the UK market during the remainder of the century are already in existence in various foreign markets today.

COMPETING THROUGH QUALITY

'Quality' shares with 'new' and 'exciting' the unfortunate fate of being frequently used to describe things that aren't.

In this book 'quality' is used to describe every attribute, physical or psychological, of every part of a company's product offering as perceived by customers and would-be customers. That perceptibility by customers is crucial. If we are talking about any aspect of a product offering which customers do not perceive, then we are not talking about quality.

Quality has two distinctly different components. Suppliers should never lose sight of the very different nature of those components, and customers ideally should never be aware of the difference. Let me explain.

The first component of quality is how a product offering is intended to perform as a provider of customer benefits. The design of products, their formulation and specifications, their minimum output and the maximum variances in that output, their availability, pricing, delivery and servicing are all planned in a particular way to meet specific customer expectations. We shall call this component the *designed* quality. That designed quality is marketing-led and a marketing responsibility. If the marketing skill behind a designed quality of a product offering has been up to scratch, then the customer will consider that quality as very acceptable, and competitiveness, part 1, has been achieved.

An entirely different cluster of company activities is concerned with the other component of quality: *delivering the goods*. The design has to be matched by the company's actual performance. The customer has every right to expect delivered quality to be equal to designed quality. As I said earlier, customers are not concerned with and should not even notice any difference between designed and delivered quality. Addressing precisely this point, James D. Robinson, CEO of American Express, said: 'We have a two part pledge to our customers: first, only to promise what we can deliver; second, to deliver what we promise'. The practice of some companies who dodge the issue by being deliberately vague about designed quality is an admission of uncompetitivess, since the very purpose of unambiguousness and accuracy about the designed quality is to establish the competitve platform.

The delivered quality is only partly a marketing responsibility. One would expect marketing people to be held responsible for wrong sales estimates (leading to wrong stock and production levels), mixed up delivery schedules, careless sales-channel choices, or grumpy service staff, but mistakes in such other areas as manufacturing, procurement, staffing or sourcing have to be reconciled with marketing through general management, which is why competitiveness can only be built if it is company-wide as well as customer-orientated.

Companies differ in whether their competitiveness is designed-quality-led or delivered-quality-led. A few manage to achieve both. There is one powerful additional argument in favour of measures to improve delivered quality levels: it cuts cost. By making an organization delivered-quality-conscious, you reduce production hold-ups, reruns and the requirement for inspectors; and you save vast amounts by cutting out waste, sub-standard stock and reworking. Most important of all, you lose fewer customers. Douglas Danforth, Chairman of Westinghouse Electric, says: '(Our quality programme) focuses on meeting customer requirements as a top priority. In the definition of customer we include our employees because they are both suppliers to and customers of each other in the internal operations of the business'.

The most important aspect when setting a programme of competitive improvements in train in a company is to bear in mind the great difference between designed and delivered quality. They are tackled by different people doing quite different things over quite different time-spans.

MISTAKING OPERATIONS-BASED COMPETITION FOR STRATEGIC COMPETITION

A quite frightening number of businessmen do not understand the difference between operational choices and strategic choices. So when it comes to defining how you compete, those managers will try operational measures to fill a strategic void.

A very typical example is the company selling, say, carpets. The company discovers that its sales are sluggish and the trade association says that imports are increasing. 'We'll soon see about that!' the managing director says, and he sets in motion a cost-cutting programme in the factory and an incentive scheme for the sales force whereby they can earn substantial bonuses every month their sales exceed those of the corresponding month of the previous year. The cost-cutting programme succeeds and it is decided to reduce prices of many lines 'to get the stuff moving again'. Nothing much moves, however, except salesmen into the sales manager's office complaining that their earnings are down (there is no increase in the square yardage of product sold, prices are down and so therefore are commissions earned). Things for the company have got worse rather than better. The company has failed to answer strategic questions – because it never asked them in the first place. The company has made operational changes which have done nothing to either the trade or consumers except provide them with food for the thought 'Prices down, ah – quality must have been reduced too!'

The company has done nothing to size up its strategic competitive position. It was unaware that new floor-covering materials made with unconventional technologies were beginning to find their way into other parts of the house than the kitchens and bathrooms for which they had originally been intended. It was unaware that younger households were becoming increasingly conscious of matching floor coverings with wallpaper, curtains and furniture, and consequently were moving from traditional carpet shops to larger multi-purpose stores. It was unaware of the circumstance that, with increasing spending power and knowledge, consumers were more willing to spend on quality if that meant better appearance longer. Finally, the company had failed to notice that much of the maligned imports were of non-traditional design, with many of those designs being made available in a range of colour settings. The company's managing director has made a totally arbitrary guess about his company's competitive position and, as it happens, taken just about the worst decision he could have taken.

Because this kind of error occurs so often and ignores so fundamental an issue, here is another example. A company's managing director is beginning to worry about the increasing number of instances where the company's salesmen are dismissed by customers without an order. The MD requires feedback from the sales force and for 2 weeks all salesmen are required to record and report the not-to-buy arguments as and when they occur. Several hundred incidents are reported and the results tabulated. It turns out that the most frequently recurring not-to-buy arguments are:

1. Inadequate margins given.

2. Inadequate promotion and advertising support.

3. Too many late or badly timed deliveries.

4. Declining sales of product category.

Plans to revise margins and increase advertising and promotional spending are well advanced when the suggestion to take a dispassionate look at the strategic aspects of the company's competitive position is made. It is discovered, first, that the not-to-buy arguments which had been so dutifully recorded had been given not so much to reflect the truth but for their general efficacy in halting the advances of salesmen – any salesmen! It was then discovered that the market showed good growth but that the company was not sharing in that growth because it had failed to take seriously the emergence and rapid growth of a premium segment of the market characterized by imaginative product formulations and fanciful packaging. Competitors with an entry in this segment were succeeding in getting their more traditional, mainstream products to ride along in the innovative excitement. Suppliers who had not joined the bandwagons, such as our company, were being left out in the cold. There was nothing wrong with our company's margins. The promotion and advertising expenditure to sales ratio was, in fact, ahead of most competitors, but there was nothing very interesting to promote or advertise.

In this example and attempt had been made to get at causes, but the wrong investigators had been used (like Louis XV's queen, who never acquired the reputation of being the most objective judge of the character of Madame de Pompadour). When a more objective, strategically orientated assessment was made, it became possible to design an entirely different competitive approach.

KNOWLEDGE

There are three chapters in this book about knowledge (8, 9 and 10). They were written because knowledge has gained importance as a tool. I would not argue with anyone who proclaimed that knowledge is *the* most important marketing tool. Knowledge would not have gained that prominence if it weren't for its value in a company's competitive armoury. A product-development man, a promotions or advertising man, a distribution manager, a sales serviceman or – above all – a salesman who is fully briefed on every aspect of his own and each of his competitors' marketing-mix activities is more competitive than anyone who is less fully briefed. There is a very simple and very powerful reason for this: the fully briefed man can always find more and more convincing aspects in terms of which his company's product offering is better than a competitor's than the less well briefed man. For an example, over the page is a caricature. See how Citroën used what it knew about some of its 'competitors' to sell the longest-lived model of them all.

Now let me give a very simple example of how lack of knowledge makes you do stupid, uncompetitive, counter-productive things. At Van Houten, in one of our main markets, we sold a range of chocolate products. In every product category the market breakdown between milk and plain chocolate hovered around the 70/30 mark. Product categories with a young user profile had a slight milk chocolate bias and those with an older user profile a slight plain chocolate bias – nowhere more than 5 per cent away from that 70/30 ratio. We also made a chocolate-based grocery product which we knew to be popular with children. We knew the size of that market (10,000t) but not its milk/plain breakdown. We assumed it to be between 70/30 and 75/25.

Our sales were badly out of line and so we gave our sales force the facts, urged them to sell more of the milk-chocolate product, gave them extra incentives, ran promotions, talked about milk chocolate in our ads and redesigned our packs to show the product more clearly. We didn't get very far. After a year we were selling 2,800 tons of milk-chocolate product and 2,900 tons of plain.

Then at a sales conference a young salesman said that his uncle worked for one of the big grocery chains and that they sold far more plain- than milk-chocolate products. We did a simple little piece of research. What came up is shown in Table 16.1.

Nearly two-thirds of the market was in the plain-chocolate variety. With a share of 57 per cent of the market, we had been foolishly

FASTER THAN A FERRARI.
Travelling flat out at 71.5mph the Citroën 2CV will easily overtake the Ferrari Mondial travelling at 65mph.

AS MANY WHEELS AS A ROLLS ROYCE.
The £55,240 Rolls-Royce Silver Spirit. How many wheels? Four. The £2,584 Citroën 2CV. How many wheels? Exactly the same.

MORE ROOM THAN A PORSCHE.
With a possible 30cu. ft. boot space there's no need for one of those plastic luggage racks on our little run-about.

THE £2,584 CITROËN 2CV.
All you'll ever need in a car.

Citroën 2CV.

TABLE 16.1

	Market (tons)	Our sales (tons)
Milk-chocolate product	3,500	2,800
Plain-chocolate product	6,500	2,900
	10,000	5,700

hammering away at the milk-chocolate sector where there was only another 7 per cent of market share to be gained, instead of majoring on the plain-chocolate part of the market where another 36 per cent of market share was to be contested for.

USING THE WHOLE MIX

You compete with a product offering not just with a product-for-a-price. Chapter 4 talks about the marketing mix. Every single part of that mix is part of the competitive product offering to customers. Every single part of that mix therefore has the ability to make or break the competitive positioning of the company, brand or product. None should ever be overlooked; no possible combination (mix) should fail to be considered.

Customers buy benefits. Customers are extraordinarily astute buyers and very capable of weighing perceived attributes against price and of trading off perceived attributes against one another. Customers are quite willing to accept certain less favourable attributes in a product offering if there are others which are outstandingly favourable. Competitive positioning means that the marketer has discovered precisely which attributes of his product offering carry such weight among which groups of (would-be) customers that they will compensate for other attributes through which he is uncompetitive.

The most profitable food retailer in the UK attains its almost unassailable position despite having only around 250 shops, poor parking facilities, a tiny product range, only one brand, bare shelves on Monday mornings, a clinical ambience in its stores, a miniscule advertising budget and very high prices. That retailer is Marks & Spencer. Strengths are very high perceived delivered quality, a highly innovative range of fresh convenience products, highly trained and motivated staff, and very clean and orderly merchandising.

The past 11 years have shown an increase of six and a half times in the real consumer value of food and drink from Germany imported into the UK. Most products initially carried unknown (and unpronounceable) brand names. Few had been reformulated to 'suit the British taste'. Quite a few in fact were types of product unfamiliar and unrecognizeable among British consumers. Nearly all were expensive and not widely available. Advertising expenditure was extremely low. Germany is not known among Britons as the origin *par excellence* of food and drink beyond sausages, lager beer and white wine. The German products sold on their high perceived delivered quality, on the prestige their use afforded, on the type of shops through which they were sold and on the skilful tenacity of those (mostly agents/ distributors) who sold them.

My final example is where the marketing mix was *not* used in a competitive situation which I witnessed. A professional fisherman was extending his fleet. Building had started and the stage had come where a choice of engines had to be made. There was a short-list of two from different makers. The two engines offered near equality in performance, specifications, servicing requirements, technical reputation, and price. Our fisherman then asked each maker: 'Tell me why I should choose your product in preference to all others?'

Manufacturer A thereupon produced detailed data on small advantages in operating performance, reliability and durability of his product and demonstrated the excellent capabilities of the local service agent. Manufacturer B said they were 'the oldest and most reputable' in the industry and had the most extensive dealer network in the country.

One of the main concerns of our fisherman (I imagine, of any fisherman), working with crews who are not engineers, was reducing the hazard of engine failure when out at sea. With the knowledge he had been given he ordered from manufacturer A.

It was several months later that I discovered that manufacturer B offered, with every engine sold and free of charge, a truly superb training programme specifically geared to the non-engineer small-boat operator to teach him servicing, preventive maintenance, simple repairs and 'get-you-home' measures. I have not the slightest doubt that failure to reveal this uniquely competitive ingredient in his product offering lost B the business.

Attached to all or any of the marketing-mix ingredients are further factors which help to fortify a competitive positioning. Speed, flexibility, interpersonal skills, professionalism, and information are examples of a list which could probably be extended endlessly.

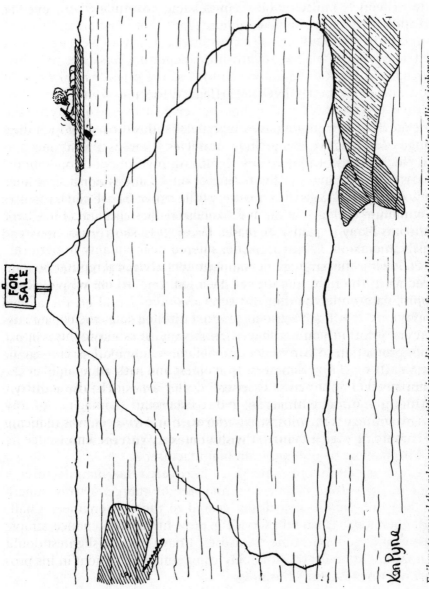

Failure to reveal the relevant competitive ingredient comes from talking about tips when you're selling icebergs.

I have pointed out that competitive strengths in certain competitive ingredients can compensate for weaknesses in others. This does not mean that downright failures in certain areas (product breakdowns, late deliveries, faulty invoices, misleading advertising) can ever be compensated for or should be tolerated.

DOING NOTHING WRONG

The previous paragraphs have suggested that there is an almost endless range of alternative competitive strategies. There is a final one. It is simple, it does not require any significant investment in operational assets or any changes in the nature of the business, nor does it need new operational skills. It carries very little risk of failure and it requires a minimum of imagination. It is likely to reduce cost and at the same time it is likely to justify increased prices. It is also very obvious and easily understood: *Don't do anything wrong*.

Following this strategy, a company will always produce the right product in the right quantity at the right time. It will supply all the appropriate outlets within the agree delivery period on the agreed conditions. It will advertise its product offering so as to activate customers, inform them and never irritate any of its publics. It will use sales promotion to win new customers or to stimulate greater usage among its existing customers. In its relations with all its publics the company will come across as appealing and honest. The company will do all those things without fail and consistently.

This strategy is the most straightforward and most successful means of competing ever invented. I wish you every success with it!

Index